The Yorkshire Organic Gardener

Graham Porter

Best wishes

Graham P.

Published by D&M Heritage Press

First published 2018

Text and images © Graham Porter

The moral right of author name to be identified as the author of
this work has been asserted.

Publisher: Jeremy Mills

Design: Dawn Cockcroft
         Harry Morris

Project Manager: Jo Dyrlaga

ISBN: 978-1-911148-24-1

Contents

Introduction

SOME YEARS AGO, I realised that the process of gardening had become, like the rest of our modern society, a more and more complicated affair. A strange thing, considering that we are always being told about low maintenance gardens, easier to use tools, one off mulches, one off lawn treatments and much, much more that is supposed to give us more leisure time. It is a little like computerised tills in shops - have you checked how long it takes to process your purchases these days as compared with an old-fashioned mechanical till - come back Mr Arkwright (Ronnie Barker), all is forgiven? For that matter, how long do we have to wait these days in a queue for a decent cup of coffee?

Not only do we now have more new varieties of plants coming out each year (the supposed 'must have list' named after wanabee celebrities, who will almost certainly be forgotten long before the plant is) to make us collect plants, that after two or three years have been replaced by another batch of 'different' plants, but we also have new technology, creating machinery that has more buttons and levers that any one person can cope with and more companies providing garden ornaments, garden design features and 'must have' extras than there are empty clothes shops on the high street. I suppose that this has been going on since our current consumer society started in Victorian times but it does seem to have become an art form now.

So, for those of us that are lucky enough to live in semi-detached suburbia and have our own little piece of Yorkshire to play with, what is it that we are all striving for when we dash to the local garden centre, supermarket, DIY shed, plant sale or open garden with a plant table, or internet buy-on-line website?

Are we trying to keep up with the Jones' or are we trying to be the Jones, for everyone else to keep up with? Whichever category you feel that you fit into, I hope that by the time you have dipped into some or all of the following chapters and their associated appendices, you will have decided that, either you would be better off living in a flat with three or four houseplants and a couple of window boxes for your horticultural indulgence, or you will be rethinking the way that you use and manage your few square metres of Planet Earth.

By the way, having practiced gardening and professional horticulture since 1966, I know now that I have changed my way of thinking and behaving in the garden at least three times since my career got underway and it may well change again before I cast off this mortal coil. This may be to do with trends, wisdom, age or energy levels but each change has got me closer to writing this book and I hope that you enjoy reading the following pages as much as I have enjoyed writing them. For your information, I have tried to use metric measurement throughout this book because I feel that it is time a book was written without the annoying and unnecessary conversions back into our confusing and somewhat primitive imperial measurements. I have also tried to use the correct and hopefully up-to-date and internationally accepted botanical names for plants as much as possible, because the vernacular, often local names for plants are too many and varied across the British Isles and beyond to be of any real horticultural value.

For any inconsistencies in plant names, blame the Botanists and Taxonomists in the Angiosperm Phylogeny Group as they and others around the world revisit the work of Linnaeus and others with their newly found genetic knowledge, gained from the various genome projects over recent years. Genetic fingerprinting and DNA sampling are not just used by the National Health Service and the Police Authorities - agriculturists, botanists, horticulturists, marine biologists, taxonomists and zoologists have all take this newly developed science on-board. The latest confirmed plant names can be found at www.theplantlist.org with all the old synonyms there to help you search for the latest Genus or species name.

Finally, of all the prose, poetry and quotations that I have searched for and used in writing this, my first book, the poet, philosophy and writer Thomas Moore has given me a quote from his book *The Re-enchantment of Everyday Life* that could not describe any better what I want this book to say:-

> *'The garden reconciles human art and wild nature, hard work and deep pleasure, spiritual practice and the material world. It is a magical place because it is not divided. The many divisions and polarizations that terrorize a disenchanted world find peaceful accord amongst mossy rock walls, rough stone paths, and trimmed bushes. Maybe a garden sometimes seems fragile, for all its earth and labor, because it achieves such an extraordinary delicate balance of nature and human life, naturalness and artificiality. It has its own liminality, its point of balance between great extremes.'*

Graham Porter
June 2018

Chapter One

Organic Gardeners and Gardening

Oh, Adam was a gardener, and God who made him sees
That half the proper gardener's work is done upon his knees,
So when your work is finished, you can wash your hands and pray
For the Glory of the Garden that it may not pass away!

Rudyard Kipling (1865–1936)
From: The Glory of the Garden (1911)

IF WE ALL want to be gardeners, or dare I say, think that we already are, I feel that we should try to identify some, if not all, of the properties that make a person into a gardener and a small piece of land into a garden - then we can make our own minds up about whether we have achieved Gardener status, or not!

We can search around for cartoon images of old men with straw hats, a pipe and dirty wellies or we can call in at our local allotment site and gather generic images of the eclectic mix of people that you will see there. We can visit our local park and look for people in green overalls or call in at our local nursery and find the owner with an apron on. Unfortunately, none of these images will provide you with the absolute picture of a real gardener because it is not what we see of the person that matters, necessarily, but what we see of the results of their horticultural work.

And before you start conjuring up your own images of a beautiful garden or for that matter a beautiful gardener, it is not necessarily a stripped lawn with clipped edges or a border full of extravagant flowers from January to December.

A general view of the back corner of my garden in early May, showing a mixed planting style that tries to provide some colour and interest throughout the seasons. By the way, the Heron is plastic!

I have listed below my own top nine factors that I feel make up an Organic Gardener and his / her garden. I wonder if you can add your own ideas. Answers on a postcard please.

1. Organic Gardeners are people who understand the complex relationship between the managed space of a garden and the natural world around it. (Ecology - the balance of nature, minimalist gardening)

2. Organic Gardeners know, despite their best efforts, that the natural cycles of weather and season will, ultimately, determine how successful their gardening is. (Hardiness, Rainfall, Wind speed and direction, Cold weather, Sunshine, Microclimate, Soil type etc)

3. Organic Gardeners will understand and be able to manage the often-long time scales of plant development that allow for the longer term development of the garden rather than the transitory use of wow factor plants. (Plant choice, plant knowledge, pruning, evolution etc)

4. Organic Gardeners will create a green space that is harmonious and fits with its surroundings as well as providing space and facilities for the gardener and their family. (Design)

5. Organic Gardeners have a natural ability to know when and how to increase the good plants and get rid of the bad ones. (Propagation and weed control)

6. Organic Gardeners have a good understanding of the complex materials that we call soils and composts and the vital part they play in the success of our gardens and our crops. (soil and water management)

7. Organic Gardeners will try to avoid the commercialism of modern gardening and only buy according to need. (the garden shed and all the tools and equipment required).

8. Organic Gardeners are able to accept that, when a plant has failed to perform or has finished performing, it can make excellent compost. (composting, pest and disease control)

9. Organic Gardeners will only choose to use hard structures in the garden if they enhance their ability to grow good plants or to use the space in the garden more affectively. (paths, patio, fences, glasshouses etc

Each of these nine ideas can be looked at in isolation and will form the basis of the following chapters in the book, although Organic Gardeners will use them all together to create and care for the Yorkshire Organic Garden.

Chapter 2

The Link Between the Garden and the Natural World

A garden is but nature debauched.

Henry David Thoreau (1817-1862)

IF GARDENERS CANNOT remember anything else, they should remember that, at the moment they think they have 'controlled' some noxious weed, infectious disease or rampaging pest, another unwanted and often unexpected invader leaps over the garden wall and attacks their favourite plants. Thus, the closer your garden is, in the way it is planted and managed, to the natural world that it sits in, the less likely you are to notice, when those small armies of invaders decide that your garden is more tasty than the wilder landscape, or even the garden next door. In fact, you should reach the point of being able to ignore the large majority of the problems because you begin to understand how the balance of nature works. Step in with a herbicide, insecticide, fungicide or any other poisonous man-made concoction and you immediately upset that delicate balance, developed over hundreds if not thousands of years, and then have to face the consequences, as some unseen pest has a population explosion because you have just inadvertently killed its only parasite, predator or pathogen with some noxious man-made chemical or, more worryingly, because the pest has become resistant to many of the current supply of pesticides. The medical world has finally realised that the continued use of anti-biotics for a variety

A cluster of yellow ladybird's eggs waiting to hatch and predate on the leaf-curling plum aphid. A perfect example of leaving the garden to find its own balance.

of human and animal ailments is no longer sustainable - the agricultural and horticultural profession has been facing this scenario for over 40 years as pests, even weeds and diseases have developed complete or partial resistance to the man-made chemical concoctions produced since the 1950s!

The question for all gardeners, and those who are seeking to be gardeners, is how can you achieve an ecological balance whilst still producing a garden that is colourful, productive and functional?

I have struggled with this complex issue since moving to a new house and garden, 200 metres up in the Pennines south of Huddersfield and, despite my hard work and continuous studies and observations, I still do not feel that I have achieved the final goal of total harmony between my garden and the natural world that it sits in - perhaps I never will!

However, during the struggle, I have discovered many interesting facts and ideas that make the waiting worthwhile. I hope that you enjoy reading through some of the techniques that I have used to help develop a garden that has a place for plants, animals, birds, insects, fungi and any other wild living organisms that decide to make my garden their home, however temporary or permanent.

STONE PILES

Living in West Yorkshire as I do, you can imagine that I am surrounded by dry stone walls, stone quarries, rocky outcrops, stone buildings and of course the Pennines (the longest stone pile in Britain).

I learnt, many years ago, as a young, inquisitive boy, that, if you turn a stone over, you are likely to find several 'creepy crawlies' underneath, many of which have a turn of speed that Lewis Hamilton would be proud of. These speed merchants are usually the predators, such as centipedes and ground beetles. The sluggish ones (yes, that is where the word comes from) are mostly vegetarian, chasing food sources that cannot move, and therefore are potential problems for those of us that insist on choosing *Hostas, Lactuca* (Lettuce), *Tagetes* (Marigolds) and other susceptible plants for our gardens that slugs seem to adore. I did not know it at the time but these two distinct groups of creatures live in the same dark, damp environment because one feeds on the other. Ground beetles and centipedes actually feed on the very small slugs and their eggs, thus stopping them from getting to adulthood and causing more damage as well as starting up the next generations. Leaf, stem, flower and root eating caterpillars and larvae fit into the same category of course but are predated upon by other speedy predators and parasites.

If you are lucky enough to have a drystone wall as part of your garden, you will have one of the best forms of slug prevention, but you can simulate the effect by creating small piles of stones, bricks, and other coarse, inert materials in the quieter, and, if you prefer, unseen corners of the garden. They do not need to be miniature mountains and can be made into ornamental or even architectural features if you wish but the benefits will be the same, however many and sizable they are. I have observed, at night, small armies of slugs emerging from these piles and they are followed by the army of predators. Remember that you will never win the war against slugs and snails, but you might, with the help of these predators, win one or two battles. You should also be aware that snails like to hibernate in large clusters in the nooks and crannies of stone walls and stone piles as well as under the dense foliage of certain garden plants - use their diurnal resting places and winter hibernation as opportunities to gather a few up and deal with them!

Views down part of Nidderdale between Harrogate and Pateley Bridge.

Littondale, showing the glacially worn valleys and a section of those wonderful drystone walls.

Snails are mostly nocturnal and return to their diurnal resting locations every morning. A perfect way of managing these annoying and sometimes devastating molluscs is to find these resting places and pick up a handful They use the same locations over winter.

Keep in mind that since the invention of Metaldehyde based slug pellets, the slug and snail problem for gardeners and growers seems to have increased proportionately - make your own mind up about that!

Log Piles

If you ever do any pruning of larger woody subjects in your garden, the chances are that, if you are a more traditional gardener, you will set fire to them, releasing large quantities of carbon unnecessarily into an already overloaded atmosphere. If you are of a more modern bent, you may, like me, take the prunings to your local household waste recycling centre for shredding and composting or you may shred them yourself for use as a mulch after they have been composted.

However, with some of your larger woody pieces, why not create a log pile in a quiet corner of the garden that will help to further develop habitats for predatory creatures as part of the 'balance of nature' in your garden. If you have an artistic leaning you can make the log pile into an ornate garden feature or, if you want to further develop 'habitats' for wildlife, why not build a 'home' for a hedgehog in the stack.

Of course, unlike the stone pile, the log pile will slowly rot away, being eaten by a wide variety of creatures and saprophytic fungi, until it crumbles into dust and gets absorbed back into your garden soil. By that time you will probably have built another one in a different part of the garden. The creatures and fungi helping with this valuable work will of course become food for another part of a connected food web, thus helping the carbon and nitrogen cycles to continue. This technique is being used widely in the management of woodland, old railway tracks and nature reserves to help support any living organism that finds this type of environment suitable.

Log piles are a beneficial way of using your woody waste from the garden that does not involve noisy shredders or trips to the tip. Insects, small mammals, bacteria and fungi will use the timber and the shelter to help complete their life-cycles and add to the biological diversity of your garden. One of the many log piles along the Trans Pennine Trail between Penistone and Dunford Bridge.

Hedging your Bets

Cast your eyes around any local natural woodland and you will see a mix of tree and shrub species forming different nesting, feeding and sheltering layers and effects and, because of the diversity, supporting a wide range of creatures and other vital living organisms, both seen and unseen.

The average hedge in the suburban gardens of Britain tends to be mono-species, often evergreen and frequently coniferous. This species choice is not only boring for the owner and a potential nuisance for the neighbours but does not support a lot of wildlife as a result, apart from an occasional nesting bird or an army of invading Cypress aphids - these are the pests that are slowly but surely killing off the dreaded Leyland cypress, *Cupressus x leylandii*. The 'High Hedges' legislation, that battled its way through the British Parliament in the early part of the 21st Century, may have some longer-term benefits as people are encouraged to reduce or remove these alien hybrid monsters from the British landscape and replace them with a more acceptable mix of native and/ or ornamental species.

My mixed hedge on the Eastern boundary of my garden, with Holly, Field Maple, Beech, Hawthorn and Dog Rose to add colour, texture and interest to the garden.

Choose the right mix and balance of species and a hedge can become one of the most valuable wildlife features of any garden. It becomes a miniature, linear woodland, supporting a vast array of macro and micro-organisms, from birds and bees to butterflies and bugs. Choose the right species and you will only have to cut the hedge once a year (a good thing in any gardeners' book)! See Appendix 1 for some more thoughts on hedges.

My own boundary hedge started life as a collection of two-year-old whips (seedling trees) planted as a double staggered row. I used *Acer campestre* (Field Maple), *Fagus sylvatica* (Beech) and *Crataegus monogyna* (Hawthorn) when we moved into our current house in the early 1980s and within two years had a hedge that reached some 2 metres high and is now a solid barrier cut in an A shape with a wide base and a narrower top to make it stronger in periods of heavy snowfall and to make the hedge a more attractive place for the various forms of wildlife that choose to use it for shelter, protection, feeding and breeding. Since planting, I have seen *Ilex aquifolium* (Holly) and *Rosa canina* (Dog Rose) appear in the hedge through bird dropped seed and this extra diversity has helped the hedge to provide more support and feeding of the wildlife in the garden. The hedge bottom has become a linear stone pile over the years, as garden developments and changes have exposed fist sized pieces of the local, rather crumbly sandstone, supporting a wide range of insects and birds as well as allowing me to let nettles and other wild plants grow in a natural, undisturbed situation so that they can in turn support an active population of British native butterflies and other creatures. A similar effect can be created with a well planted, mixed, relatively undisturbed shrubbery, although you may choose not to have the nettles in an ornamental border. The hedge provides a feeding site for fungi, insects and birds or all shapes and sizes, up to top predators such a sparrow hawks - regular visitors to the garden in the hunt for a quick meal off an unwary sparrow - a complex food web that manages itself and provides the gardener with the additional pleasure of watching it evolve and watching the individual players taking part.

TO FEED OR NOT TO FEED

Although I realise that, in the rather false circumstances of the vegetable garden and the container garden, the use of fertilisers, whether organic or otherwise, is essential; this is only because the techniques of growing are entirely unnatural, therefore requiring unnatural, measured attention to ensure some level of success.

Walk to your local woodland or onto a local, natural hillside and ask yourself when it was that someone took a bag of fertiliser to feed the trees, grasses and wild flowers. The answer is that no one ever did and, in fact, it would be very damaging if they did. The natural cycles of defecation, death and decomposition by every living creature, as well as plant decomposition, recycle all the available nutrients that the resident population of plants require and thus a balance is struck between the living and the dead. Whether you study the Water cycle, the Carbon cycle or the Nitrogen cycle, the results are just the same - vast quantities of naturally occurring minerals are recycled and released as every plant and creature casts off its waste products and finally its mortal coil.

In our gardens this does mean allowing autumn leaf fall to happen without too much of our intervention so that the goodness from the leaves of deciduous shrubs and trees can be recycled by the worms, bacteria and fungi. More of this in Chapter 7, when I take a look at soils and in Chapter 9 when I look at the apparently complex subject of composting. I only remove leaves from the lawn, to avoid an excessive build up of earth worms, from the pond to prevent a stinking, anaerobic sludge from developing and encouraging algal blooms from forming at the first sign of any spring sunshine, and from paths to stop me (or any member of my family) from slipping down the garden path as I take the morning constitutional around my 'estate.' I will also clear leaves away from emerging spring bulbs and Hellebores to avoid etiolation of their emerging flowers and foliage. These are then added to the compost heap, piled up under the hedge or scattered beneath one of the shrubs, where they decompose at their own speed, providing further feeding opportunities for birds and insects as well as the plants. Have you ever watched a blackbird flicking leaves out of the way in his or her search for a juicy worm or other hidden treat? That is a good enough reason to leave most of the leaves where they fall.

With a successful compost heap, your garden will produce most of the organic matter that you need for soil improvement during ground preparation for sowing or planting. Larger quantities and woody waste can now be recycled through the many successful local authority green waste recycling systems. As I do not own a shredder, I use this system for disposing of bulky woody waste from trees, the hedges and shrub pruning that are not needed for the building of another log pile. I add shredded personal and business papers to the compost heap to add bulk and carbon to the wet, nitrogen laden, green garden and vegetative kitchen waste - a resident family of field mice like it for nesting in as well!

WATER, WATER EVERYWHERE!

From the end of the 20th Century to the early part of the 21st Century, since the advent of garden makeover programmes on television, every gardener seems to think that the garden cannot do without an ornamental water feature. Bubble fountains, rills, miniature canals, dribbling globes, Japanese tipping bamboo water features, water cascades, fountains and lots of other variations have become 'must have' additions to the garden, many needing electrical filters and pumps to help manage the water quality or speed. Water features in the wild do not have any of this technology and yet they do not seem to suffer from blanket weed, algal blooms or other invasive problems requiring modern technology to sort them out.

The Yorkshire Organic Gardener will know why and will create a water feature that benefits the garden and the natural world without increasing atmospheric pollution by burning a small power station's worth of electricity as the pumps work at keeping your water clean and circulating 24 hours a day.

A wildlife pond can, once established, almost manage itself, leaving you time to enjoy the comings and goings of a wide variety of wild creatures, from wasps taking a quick drink whilst balanced on a Nymphaea (Water Lily) leaf, to a Smooth Newt popping its head up for a gasp of air.

See Chapter 5 for some thoughts on garden ponds, their design and location in a good wildlife garden.

One of the simplest and yet most essential water features in any garden is a well placed and routinely maintained bird bath. Placed in a quiet corner away from human disturbance and topped up as a often as necessary (up to three times a day in summer in my garden), this feature not only provides the birds with the necessary drinking and washing facilities but also encourages birds into your garden. Placed near a large shrub, small tree or hedge where the birds can finish off their preening and drying out, this cheap garden feature will give you hours of harmless fun observing the antics of different birds as they complete their toilet and take a well earned drink, even in the depths of winter!

You must ask yourself whether you want a water feature for you to enjoy or for the wildlife to benefit from; or might it be that both parties can be satisfied. Personally, I am not interested in my 'hole in the ground with water in it' being an extravagant ornamental feature with lots of beautiful flowers and large fish. It, like natural water features, supports a population of various amphibians, insects and molluscs, provides drinking and bathing opportunities for birds and animals and, if I am lucky, gives me the bonus of a display of water irises and water lilies in season. I get more pleasure from watching damsel flies and dragonflies emerging and listening to the frogs croaking than I do from staring open mouthed at a newly opened water lily flower or watching the same gold fish or 'valuable' Koi Carp go round the pond for the thousandth time.

The other side to the water story that is so vital to the survival of plant life is the availability and delivery of the right amount of water to the right plant in the right season and at the right time of day.

The Organic Gardener will have ensured that he / she has a guaranteed supply of water from a variety of sources, whether that be a number of water butts gathering rain water from the house, sheds and glasshouses, a submerged grey water tank or a mains supply. The difference between these sources can have a major impact on a plant's chances of survival. Rain water is, by and large, much softer (neutral to acid) than tap water, particularly for those living in hard water areas and so is good for watering containerised Ericaceous plants such as Camellias and Rhododendrons. In West Yorkshire, the large majority of us have mains water that is taken from reservoirs fed by moorland water and so is very soft. Keep these potential differences in mind when you are watering plants that have a pH preference one way or another. The other factor about rain water is that it can carry spores of the various 'damping off' diseases, particularly if the rain butt does not have a cover or lid to prevent infected material from blowing or dropping in. Preferably, do not water seedlings and young susceptible plants with rain water. If you are lucky enough to have house plants or a collection of glasshouse plants, it is important to remember to temper the rain or tap water to the ambient temperature of the glasshouse or room so that your plants do not get a nasty shock when you water them - a full watering can should be kept in the glasshouse at all times to ensure that it is at the right temperature - this is particularly important if you need to water plants in winter - think what it might feel like if and when you choose to take a cold shower!

The timing of the watering of your seedlings, pot plants and garden containers may seem to be an irrelevance but, if you are a hungry slug or snail that has just woken up from your diurnal snooze, the smell of water will be an immediate attraction - for us gardeners, this gives us three good reasons not to water at dusk. Firstly, it attracts those molluscan enemies. Secondly, the plants will not be using much of that water until the sun comes up the following morning, by which time some of it will have drained away and thirdly, that cool water poured onto the top and root growth may, in some cases, encourage fungal pathogens to start their evil work. Early morning watering avoids all of these problems and is a good excuse to survey your estate at a time of day when there is nobody else to disturb you.

LUXURY LAWNS

The lawn has been an important feature of British gardens for centuries and, since Edwin Budding invented the lawn mower in 1830, it has kept every 'man of the house' occupied on a Sunday afternoon, cutting, edging, scarifying, and spiking. Add the expensive spreading of the annual dressing of feed, weed and moss kill preparations of recent years and the male of the species can be satisfied that he is doing his bit or, if not, at least avoiding the Sunday lunch washing up!

The lawn is not particularly easy to link with any specific wild feature apart from woodland glades, meadows, the savannahs, steppes and prairies but is, like all other garden features, a potential haven for flora and fauna. If you have ever watched a flock of starlings or rooks pecking happily at the lawn, you will realise that they are searching for the larvae of cutworm moths, chafer beetle grubs and cranefly larvae as well as the crusts that you may have thrown out and, given some good luck and persistence, they will pull out a few of them that have spent their time eating the roots of your grass. Whilst the birds are there, they may remove some of the moss for their nests and give your lawn a spike - all without any cost or effort on your part.

Look in any ordinary gardening book and you will find a chapter on lawn care that describes a huge list of 'weeds' that can invade your green sward. I have counted up to 20 different 'weeds' in my lawn and look on them as part of the rich diversity of plants that my garden can support. On the occasions when I miss out on a weekly cut and the *Taraxicum officinalis* (Dandelions and *Plantago lanceolatus* (Narrow-leaved Plantain) seed themselves, you can be assured that the local goldfinch population will be there for breakfast; the bee population (at the last count some 7 species visiting or living in my space) is very pleased when my *Prunella vulgaris* (Self-heal) flowers and the hoverflies cannot resist taking advantage of the clumps of *Bellis perennis* (Daisy) flowers that provide an important food source from March through to October - my only granddaughter also likes making daisy chains! My *Trifolium spps* (Red and White Clover) patches not only satisfy a good population of bees but also provide the lawn and the garden with a free source of nitrogen with the help of billions of Nitrogen-fixing bacteria that live in symbiosis with clover. This adaptation of the traditional 'lawn' provides me with several benefits apart from those described above. Firstly, I do not have to cut my lawn as frequently because the grass is not fed by me; secondly, I do not have the financial strain of buying fertilizers, selective herbicides and moss killers and finally, I can help my wife to wash up the Sunday lunch. In fact, I prepare and cook the Sunday lunch some weeks, giving me the opportunity to glance out of the kitchen window and see who is visiting the garden for their own version of Sunday lunch.

British 'gardeners' seem to be obsessed with ridding the lawn of anything that is not grass and the modern combination 'Weed, Feed and Moss kill' products have only further encouraged this obsession. In using these materials, the gardener will, almost certainly, be killing out untold numbers of bacteria, mycorrhiza, fungi and other living organisms that will be recycling nutrients for you free of charge. The fertiliser will be causing the grass to have mad flushes of green growth that make the grass plants susceptible to disease, often causing scorched patches due to inaccurate application methods. The worm population does not like these chemicals either as they tend to leave an acidic residue in their wake that worms do not like. The earth worm's ability to help drain your lawn is far better than any spiker and when you see a blackbird struggling to pull a worm from the lawn, you realise that everybody benefits. All you need to do is to cut the lawn with a good lawn mower and the rest will, eventually, look after itself.

Latest research into modern peat-free / municipal green waste composts has shown that residues from selective herbicides used on lawns are now finding their way, in minute quantities, through green waste composting, into our 'environmentally friendly' composts, causing devastation to some crops - you have been warned!

Because I have chosen to avoid the use of these chemicals, my lawn now has some 20 different 'wild flowers' which forces me to reduce the frequency of cutting and to increase the height of cut. Because of this change of practice, I have seen *Cardamine pratensis* (Lady's Smock or Cuckoo Flower) and *Silene flos-cuculi* (Ragged Robin) come into my 'lawn.' I now have a managed wild flower meadow without any real effort. I suspect that many of the seeds of these 'weeds' have fallen off the backs of nocturnal mammals using my garden as a toilet, feeding place or cut-through to someone else's garden.

Lawns do not have to be pristine swards with beautiful stripes to impress your neighbours. Leave 'weeds' to establish and reduce the cutting cycle to two weeks and watch the wildlife come in and join in the fun.

PLANT A TREE IN 73 AND EVERY YEAR SINCE

I am sure that many of us in the UK will remember the slogan for planting trees in 1973. Those trees will now be reaching maturity and will be providing huge benefits in the wild as well as in the garden, let alone soaking up and storing vast quantities of carbon. National Tree Week, organised by The Tree Council, has been running since 1975 and has helped to plant millions of new trees across the UK as well as investing time and money in educating children and adults about the value of trees in our world.

Because we cannot see much of what goes on in the crowns of most trees, we assume that little is happening. How wrong we are. Estimates of over 200 creatures and other life forms living in, on or under a mature Quercus (oak) tree will give you some idea of the huge diversity, with each one supporting one or more of the other creatures in a complex food web. I would not suggest that you consider planting an oak tree in a small suburban garden but there are a number of excellent trees for the small garden (see Appendix 1) that will add to the diversity of fauna that visit and live on these trees. The tree becomes a miniature woodland and provides all the wildlife benefits that several hundred hectares of woodland can provide, only on a very small scale. Birds feed on the insects, flowers, fruits and seeds, insects feed on the flowers, foliage or on other insects and the high branches provide an escape route from ground predators such as cats - an unnatural phenomenon in the garden that is disproportionately out of scale with the natural balance of top predators to primary and secondary sources of food such as birds.

On the broader environmental aspects of trees, we know that they, along with the vast peat bogs of the world, are one of the best stores of the world's surplus carbon and, with individuals, organisations and even large international companies now showing concern for their carbon footprint, it is beholding on all of us to do what we can to plant more woody subjects and to help offset the effects of the destruction of the world's woodlands and forests. We now complain about the terrible devastation of the Amazon rainforests, the destruction of huge diverse forests of Madagascar and the removal of rainforests in the Far East to make way for Palm Oil plantations, and yet our predecessors did little to stop the uncontrolled removal of our own British and European forests during the 15th to 19th century period when we were trying to rule the world. Henry V111 and his successors have a lot to answer for. In Queen Elizabeth II's Diamond Jubilee year of 2012, the Woodland Trust was endeavouring to plant 6 million trees to help celebrate her achievement but also to try and redress the imbalance that the UK has with its tree stock - we are the least treed country in Europe! Recent announcements of a Northern Forest stretching from Liverpool to Hull are welcome and, I am sure that, assuming it happens, we in Yorkshire will all benefit, in the longer term. Link up with your local branch of the Woodland Trust, who are co-ordinating this project, to find out more and to see if you and your family can help.

On a happier note, I have watched a large male Mistle Thrush totally dominate a neighbour's

This Betula utilis 'Jacqumontii' was planted by my wife and I for our 25th Wedding Anniversary in 2000 and now gives us great pleasure throughout the year as an ornamental tree and as a source of food, shelter and protection for a wide variety of wild creatures.

Sorbus aucuparia 'Joseph Rock' (Rowan), as the yellowish berries have ripened, from late October to January and have been fascinated by the number and variety of other birds that have attempted, usually unsuccessfully, to benefit from this particular natural larder. Eventually, a large flock of fieldfares, redwings or waxwings arrive and push the noisy Mistle Thrush out of the way, leaving the tree bare again for another 8 months or so. The same feeding frenzy is true on *Betula pendula* (Silver Birch), *Betula utilis* 'Jacquemontii', *Cotoneaster cornubia* and *Prunus padus* (Bird Cherry) when they produce fruits or seeds and it one of the greatest pleasures in my garden, to know that I am helping to support these wild creatures, whilst I get some pleasure from the trees as well as the birds.

FLOWER POWER

In the few truly wild areas of Britain that are left the flowers produced by soft, herbaceous plants, shrubs and trees are almost always simple, single flowers that attract pollinating insects - they have to be like this to ensure that they can be pollinated, fertilized and subsequently produce seed for the next generation. The result is lots of insects and birds and lots of wild flowers, shrubs and trees. Everyone wins!

In our modern gardens several things have happened during the plant breeding work that has been done since Georgian times. Some flowers are now producing sterile flowers that do not need to attract insects and so have lost their scent and nectar - you cannot save any seed from these and so have to go back to the suppliers every year for fresh but very expensive seeds!! The cotton farmers of India have been facing this problem for some years as they are forced to buy genetically modified sterile seed and so cannot save their own seed as their forebears have done for centuries! Many flowers are now so double that any nectar or pollen is often inaccessible to insects and so, apart from the gardener who can admire these displays of flowers. Nobody wins!

Another factor in the vast range of issues to be considered is the style and makeup of the flowers. There are number of plant families (see Appendix 1) whose flowers are particularly good at providing the nectar and pollen needed by pollinating and other beneficial creatures. These include Rosaceae (the rose family), Asteraceae syn. Compositae (the daisy family), Labiatae, syn. Lamiaceae (the dead nettle family), Scrophulariaceae (the figwort family), Leguminosae (the pea family) and Plantaginaceae (plantain family). Choose plants from these families and you can be sure to attract a wide range of insects to the flowers and, in some cases, attract larger creatures to the results of pollination in the form of seeds and berries. The insects benefit from this symbiotic relationship as the flowers provide nectar to give them energy and pollen for the essential proteins needed for egg production.

Unfortunately, many people assume that, regardless of global warming, most plants only flower from February onwards and most insects only appear at the same time as you in the garden, namely from late March through to mid-October. This is so far from the truth and, if you were one of those early flying bumble bees (as early as December according to BBC Spring Watch initiatives and various phenological statistics), you would be on the lookout for a quick sugar fix to give you the necessary energy to build your nest and start egg laying. In gardening terms, this means ensuring that your garden has some plants in flower throughout the whole year; even on the coldest days of winter. In the wild these are provided by a huge diversity of plants over large areas. In your own garden all that is required is to plant one or two good winter flowering shrubs and the bees will be happy. See my suggested plants list in Appendix 1 for some ideas and then pay a call to one or two local garden centres or nurseries from October to February, avoiding the array of Christmas displays and post Christmas sales and concentrating instead on the outdoor displays of seasonal trees, shrubs and herbaceous plants.

WHEN IS A WEED NOT A WEED?

'The Dandelion' by Richard Church (1893–1972)

I am the sun's remembrancer, the boy
Who runs in hedgerow, and in field and garden,
Showing his badge, a round-faced golden joy
With tips of flame. I bear my master's pardon
For my long, greedy roots. I bring his message
And pay his sovereign coin for my passage.
If any call me robber of the soil,
Let him but wait on windy weather, note
How easily, without a mortal's toil,
I change from my gold to silver treasure, float
The fairy mintage on the air, and then
Defy the curse of all industrious men.

Digitalis purpurea (Foxglove) and Rubus fruticosus (Blackberry) are from plant families whose flowers are designed to support pollinating insects - a typical symbiotic relationship so vital in an organic garden.

Weeds, using the human definition, do not truly exist in the wild unless they have leapt the wrong way over the garden wall - *Rhododendron ponticum, Persicaria japonica* (Japanese Knotweed), *Impatiens glandulifera* (Himalayan Balsam) and *Heracleum mantegazzianum* (Giant Hogweed) being prime examples of this process - all these and many more besides have been brought into this country, without any knowledge or understanding of the eco-systems that they are being taken from, by successive plant hunters from across the globe. As the world has, metaphorically speaking, shrunk, these problems of export or import of undesirables, has got worse. And now, as a result of this, you can walk round any garden centre in Britain and you will see a vast range of chemicals, machinery and tools, designed to keep this apparently uncontrollable army of invasive thugs at bay.

Why is it that, in the balanced garden, as in the wild, weeds do not seem to take over and certainly do not need the combined attentions of a hoe, a fork, a flame thrower and a knapsack sprayer?

Many of the so called 'weeds' can provide added benefits to the Organic Gardener and, if you read Chapter 6, you will find out the whats and whys of this fascinating aspect of gardening with nature.

See Appendix 3 Weeds for each garden situation and some ideas on how to manage them.

MONITORING SUCCESS

One of most pleasurable pastimes that I have had in my garden, as it has developed into a wildlife friendly location, is sitting, watching and researching the various phases of each creature's activities. Their arrival, if they are not resident, their searching for food, a mate or shelter, whichever one is their greatest priority, and their successful completion of a life cycle, with the next generation having been born into a garden that can support them. I have recently discovered a term to describe what I have been doing in my garden for over 30 years - Ethology - the study of the function and evolution of animal behaviour. Nice to give it a name!

For 14 years, as I watched my garden evolve from a blank canvas in the early 1980s to its semi-maturity twenty years later, I kept a random record (not in any way scientific) of those comings and goings in the garden and I still get great pleasure from reading through it to see what left a calling card in our garden during that time. I was recently gifted a wildlife camera that has added enormously to this observation process, particularly as we now have regular visits from a local badger and a fox.

Impatiens glandulifera (Himalayan Balsam), a close relative of our beloved 'Busy Lizzies', came from the foothills of the Himalayan mountains and is now classified as an invasive species in many countries across Europe, including the UK. Its annual lifecycle and explosive seed pods allows it to spread rapidly along streamsides and other damp environments, smothering everything else in its path. Rhododendrum ponticum was not recorded in the UK until the mid 18th Century and it escaped into the countryside.

Although we do not seem to have a visiting population of them in recent years, I watched 7 swallows sitting on a telephone wire on September 21st 1986 as their prepared for their long journey back to Africa. I wonder what or who has stopped this annual migration to our neighbourhood? They arrived back on April 30th 1987 by the way. After four years of garden development, I saw a small deposit of Hedgehog droppings for the first time on July 13th 1988 and have had regular visits from him / her or one of its relatives ever since, with some winters being spent under the dry foliage of a large *Cortaderia selloiana* (Pampas grass). Who needs a garden full of flowers?

When you have several years of observing the same creatures arriving or emerging at roughly the same time each year, you begin to realise that there is something about your garden that they like, even if you are not quite sure what that something might be. Look up their life cycle in a good text book (see the Bibliography for more information) and you will be able to see whether it is the plants in your garden that they are attracted to or those in next doors garden. A good example of this is the orange tip butterfly (*Anthocharis cardamines*). We have observed it in the garden and now know that it is because of a small patch of *Cardamine pratensis* (cuckoo flower or ladies smock) as one of their most popular food plants. The pupae attach themselves to the stems and twigs of a number of garden plants, not necessarily related to the food plants and, as there is only one generation a year, it would be all too easy to cut back those plants and destroy next year's butterflies without knowing.

An Orange tip butterfly taking a nectar feed from a wild vetch flower.

Gold Crests are Britain smallest birds and you will need a good pair of eyes (or binoculars) to see them flitting about in amongst shrubs and trees. I have been lucky to see them five times in the garden since 1988 and they become one of the indicators of a quiet and peaceful environment as these birds are very shy and easily disturbed.

Bumble-bees are amongst the most important pollinators for the domestic garden as they are good at random feeding and inadvertent pollination, whilst their honey-bee relatives are much more focused. Over a number of years of gradually reducing the disturbance of the garden and its soil, I have noticed a progressive increase in the population of bumble-bees and other related species in the garden and can now watch them flying to and from flowers and their underground nests in a variety of locations in the garden from January until October.

I do wonder, if we all did a little less strimming, cutting, digging, mowing and barbecuing, whether these delightful creatures might spend a little more time with us and give us more pleasure than we apparently get from this manic rush to keep our gardens neat and trim. Add to these activities things like garden lighting that confuse the nocturnal moth population and add to the light pollution that stops us seeing so many wonderful stars on a clear night, and even garden music that confuses the bird population and it is no wonder that we do not see much wildlife. Maybe it is there but we either don't have time to see it whilst we are burning another chicken wing, roasting under our patio heaters, opening another bottle of Chianti or feeding our Koi carp or, most worrying of all, we don't actually care whether it is there or not!

Biodynamics and mycorrhiza - these two re-emerging sciences are becoming more important to both amateur and commercial horticulturists, particularly those that are growing crops using organic methods. Biodynamics is a complex science using Lunar cycles, weather cycles, soil science and many other naturally occurring influences to control the timing of planting, sowing, harvesting of your crops and perhaps over the coming years, as our planet is put under increasing pressure to produce enough food to supply an ever increasing human population (7 billion in 2012), we may all need to study and understand these issues more, to ensure that we can maximise the use of every square metre of growing space.

Mycorrhiza are naturally occurring microscopic fungal organisms that have been known about for many years but modern research techniques have allowed them to be studied more closely and, for some, to be made into commercially available products for anyone growing plants. The fungi live in symbiosis with the plant's root system and help it to extract food and water better, thus reducing the need for excessive amounts of fertilizer and water. It also aids the plants natural defence mechanisms against pests and diseases. We are now able to buy planting composts and planting additives that are impregnated with these microscopic fungi to help in the establishment of new plants. One of the strange things about them is that they do not seem to be useable with any Brassica crops or Rhododendrons!

Of course, as you might imagine, being microscopic and yet complex, these mycorrhiza are sensitive to changes in all aspects of soil conditions and the addition of inorganic pesticides, fertilizers and other unnatural substances will almost certainly have a detrimental effect on them, cancelling out any benefits that we might think we have gained with these purchased products. In a healthy soil that has had plenty of organic material added by nature and the gardener, these organisms will form a natural part of the soil biota, along with fungi, bacteria, worms, beetles, centipedes and many more in numbers beyond human comprehension. Try looking up 'water bears' and see what you get. Our gardens have many millions of them in the soil water!

My studies of these subjects are still in their comparative infancy and it may well be that the next phase of my horticultural and environmental understanding and wisdom involves utilising these ancient yet modern sciences to help me manage my garden better!

Permaculture - before I outline what I think this concept is, I would suggest that you visit www.permaculture.org.uk and spend an hour reading the 12 principles and 3 ethics of this vital model for us all to seriously consider taking on board, as a whole or in part, as your current life style allows.

Permaculture is probably at the heart of what my 60,000 or so words are trying to say to all of us who have a piece of land that we chose to call a garden. Namely that we, as citizens of the world, have a responsibility to help protect and conserve the living organisms and resources of the planet for ourselves and for future generations yet to grace us with their presence.

Thus, permaculture contains more than just how to manage a plot of land in an environmentally friendly way and with the minimum impact on the planet. All other aspects of our lives should be run in an environmentally friendly way as well. Many of the modern environmental concepts that we hear almost daily in the news - reducing our energy consumption; producing, buying and using local and regional produce where at all possible; cycling or walking where at all possible; sharing what you have with those around you, whether it is goods, services, advice, practical help or friendship; growing all your food as close to the principles of organic growing as you can and reducing, reusing, reselling or recycling as much of your 'waste' as you can. You can add to the list as you find other ways of reducing your impact on the planet. Remember that, each time you take on-board a new ethic, try to encourage others to do the same. Keep words such as stability and sustainability at the forefront of your mind in all that you do and you will not go far wrong.

Forest gardening - take permaculture and give it a twist and you will come out with Forest Gardening. This concept is centred on the idea of filling your garden, as much as is feasible, with productive trees, bushes and canes, underplanted with herbs and perennial vegetables. The productivity of the plants does not

Limnanthes douglasii (Poached Egg Plant) attract bees and hoverflies in abundance.

necessarily have to be just for you and your family but also for wildlife, in all its strange and wonderful guises.

With the world continuing to tear down native trees at a faster rate than we can replant them, it is no wonder that the more environmentally enlightened amongst us are tearing our hair out by the roots.

Companion planting - knowing that, on one side of this equation, Allelopathy, the chemical inhibition of one plant (or other organism) by another is well understood, you can imagine, on the other side is the concept that growing certain plants together may be to the benefit of both. I have had a fascinating chart, created by Michael Littlewood from Somerset in my reference collection for many years and it makes excellent reading. An example to consider is the use of *Limnanthes douglasii* (Poached Egg Plant) amongst plants that are susceptible to aphid attack or require a good number of pollinators such as *Ribes rubrum* (Red Currants) - the flowers of the *Limnanthes* attract bees and hoverflies in abundance. A more obvious example is the use of leguminous crops to add Nitrogen to you soil through the wonderful process of Nitrogen fixation - it occurs in plants in the Leguminosae Syn. Fabaceae family with the aid of soil living bacteria that fix Nitrogen from the atmosphere onto the roots. These nodules then release the Nitrogen gradually over the following growing season - used widely in crop rotation and in old-fashioned pastures. See the Bibliography for details of this and the Complete Book of Companion Planting by Bob Flowerdew.

Sacrificial planting - this concept allows us to plant susceptible species of plants in our garden to attract specific pests so that they are then not encouraged to visit our more precious plants. A simple example is the use of *Tropaeolum majus* (Nasturtium) to attract Cabbage White Butterflies as far away from any Brassica crops as you can put them. Once you have a nice collection of eggs and caterpillars, you know what to do!

Chapter Three

The Ups and Downs
of Yorkshire

We may see on a spring day in one place more beauty in a wood than in any garden.

William Robinson (1838–1935)
From : The Garden Beautiful (1907)

AN OLD ANONYMOUS poem says:

> Whether the weather be fine or whether the weather be not,
> Whether the weather be cold or whether the weather be hot,
> We'll weather the weather, whatever the weather,
> Whether we like it or not.

All gardeners will know that there are only so many contraptions you can erect to protect your plants from the ravages of inclement weather before you give up and manage your garden according to the seasons, your locality and the peculiar microclimates of your own garden. This is true, no matter whether you are from Yorkshire or elsewhere!

In the natural world, plants, animals and other creatures sink or swim by the natural cycles of weather and season, one year being very successful and another year being less so - part of natural selection, if you believe what Charles Darwin (1809–1882) and Alfred Russell Wallace (1823–1913) suggested. As organic gardeners, we should accept that we will, despite all the studying, reading and discussion, also have good years and lean years; years when a shrub flowers profusely and years when it doesn't; years when we have a major slug infestation and years when we wondered what all the fuss was about; years when our apple tree produces a glut to feed the neighbourhood and years when there are barely enough apples to feed our own family.

If only we could stop trying to control nature, a strange human desire, more obvious in some people than others, and allow nature to tell us what should be done.

Since the 1970s we have all noticed a change in our climate and a gradual shift in the seasons. Spring frosts hitting our embryo Hydrangea flowers in mid-May, lawns still growing fast in November and July seeming to produce more rainfall than December. As gardeners, we cannot have much influence on these global issues but our horticultural skills and our knowledge of our own garden and its environs should help us to maximise the potential of our little piece of Planet Earth.

As an ex Boy Scout and a lover of Physical Geography at school, I have long since realised the importance of knowing where North, South, East and West are and what type of weather comes from which quarter. I was also lucky enough, when at Secondary School, to be responsible, along with a school pal, Clive Hunt, for the daily readings of our school weather station, including rainfall, sunlight hours with a Campbell Stokes Sunshine recorder, cloud type and cover, wind speed (1 - 10 Beaufort Scale readings), and, inside a Stevenson's Screen, reading a maximum / minimum thermometer and a Hygrometer (Relative Humidity). Even before my chosen career path was obvious, I was being steered in the right direction. I wonder how many schools do that type of thing these days?

Microclimates - watch your garden on a cold, frosty, winter or spring morning and see where the frost lingers and where it thaws first. Watch your garden after a summer

A Stevenson's Screen, named after the engineer and meteorologist, Sir Thomas Stevenson (1818–1887), the father of Robert Louis Stevenson (1850–1894).

thunderstorm and see where the puddles lie longest and where they dry out quickest. Realise that a good, south facing stone wall will act as a radiator in winter, pumping out its stored heat at night to protect a valuable wall-shrub from a sharp overnight frost. These indicators, and many others besides, will gradually help you draw a micro-climate map of your garden, allowing you to decide where it might be best to position certain plants, for their benefit rather than yours! Remember that this microclimate will change subtly as your garden evolves and that there are subterranean microclimates just as there are those more obvious ones above ground - if your garden seems to have a badly drained patch, rather than trying to drain it, why not take advantage of it and grow some bog plants! Solid shade created by buildings and modern garden fences, wind tunnels created by the tiny gaps between modern houses, early morning sunshine that warms on a summer morning but burns on a frosty spring morning - these are all issues that organic and natural gardeners become aware of and then garden accordingly.

Lunar cycles - watch the tide coming and going at the seaside and you will realise the incredible power of the moon, as it pulls untold trillions of litres of sea water from one side of the earth to another, and back again. This power also pulls and releases water in the soil, allowing more or less soil water to be available to plants - as the New Moon begins it cycle the sowing of seeds and the planting of plants would seem to be a good idea as more water will be available for seed germination. As the moon wanes, it is time to harvest and to weed the soil, taking advantage of the drier conditions - try it out and see what you think. Of course, when there is a full moon, it can act as a second sun during the night, reflecting the sun's light onto your plants and aiding their growth.

Day and night lengths - commercial growers have been using this strange phenomenon, known as photoperiodism, which some plants have, to give us Poinsettias at Christmas and cut flower Chrysanthemums all year round. In the garden, we cannot have any direct control over these seasonal cycles. We can of course plunge a Rhubarb crown into complete darkness for a few weeks so that we can enjoy forced Rhubarb, one of the best Yorkshire delicacies available, and we can play similar games with Asparagus, Cardooms, Celery and Endive.

I wonder if schools still teach the basics of the four seasons? The Vernal Equinox is on or around March 21st in the Northern Hemisphere after which we can enjoy three months of true spring weather and day lengths gradually extending while night lengths shrink. By the time we reach the Summer Solstice on June 21st or thereabouts, it gives us a maximum day length of up to 18 hours of day light. The shortening days from this point until September 21st, or thereabouts, take us to the Autumn Equinox when day and night length are equal once again and the following three months allow us to enjoy the autumn season, with further reducing day length and increasing night length. When we reach December 21st or thereabouts, the Winter Solstice, our day length can be down to as little as 6-7 hours, depending on your location in the British Isles, and we are thrown into three months of winter, but with gradually increasing day length as we head towards spring once again.

With a total length of around 1000km if measured in a straight line from North to South of the UK, there can be as much as two hours difference in sun rise and sun set times and this, without taking into account any other climatic or weather related details, can make a huge difference to sowing and planting times, flowering times and emergence times - beware when reading gardening books and seed packets. Consider that the first Narcissus flowers can be cut on the Scilly Isles in December and yet may not be open in the North of Scotland until February, some eight weeks later - this is of course an extreme example, but the principle is there to be noted. Being in Yorkshire, we come somewhere in the middle of these extremes and should be aware of this when working out sowing and planting times.

Prevailing wind - meteorologists will tell you that the prevailing wind direction in the UK is from the South West to the North East, giving us all a general indication of where the potentially damaging winds might come from. This allows us to plant wind-breaks, shelter belts, and hedges strategically. However, in recent years, we have had more winds from other quarters that make it necessary to shelter the whole garden. Remember the 'beast from the East' in the late winter of 2018!

Modern housing developments, with their smaller gardens, narrow passageways and larchlap fencing have increased and exaggerated this problem, scorching and damaging precious garden plants. Gardeners should remember that solid barriers such as brick walls and larchlap fencing cause an increase in wind speed and turbulence, whereas hedges and semi-permeable fencing slow down the wind, making it better for both you and your close neighbours whilst still retaining that rather strange British desire for privacy! These semi-permeable boundaries are also excellent for many forms of wildlife.

Rain fall, water tables and drainage - when I first moved to Huddersfield in 1984, having originally come from the driest part of Britain (Southend-on-Sea) with an average rainfall of 0.4 metres per annum, I was amazed to be told that it can vary from 2.0 metres per annum on Holme Moss (525 metres above sea level, to 0.8 metres in Huddersfield (150–200 metres above sea level) - this in the space of some 13 km. This incredible variation has several horticultural effects in the higher rainfall areas - lower soil temperature because of the larger volumes of water that need to be warmed up, lower average air temperature because of greater cloud cover and height above sea level, and lower light levels because of denser cloud cover and wetter soils that are not suited to all garden plants. During the initial writing of this book in 2012 the whole of the UK had been experiencing some of the wettest summer weather on record, after 20 years of below average figures in the South-East of England and has seen the effects of low light, cold soil and cooler air temperatures - more plant diseases, poor pollination because pollinating insects do not fly in these conditions, lower yields of fruit, vegetables and cereals, excessive extension growth on trees and shrubs and delayed and late harvests to name but a few.

These weather extremes have been showing up a number of anomalies that local governments, environment agencies, central government and water authorities do not seem to understand. In the days before World War II, the farming communities had ponds, ditches, dikes, drains, culverts and streams that they cared for as part of helping to keep some of their land drained, whilst other areas were allowed to hold water for animals and wildlife to drink, and yet since the war, these linear reservoirs have slowly filled in with detritus, causing roads to flood and water to find new routes to follow that we have no control over. The result of this for all of us is that crops are being ruined in the fields, road surfaces are being damaged by water and frost, with only poor attempts at repair and of course, houses and gardens are regularly going under water in the most unexpected places. It is time that the various authorities stopped wasting untold millions on extravagant flood defences and got back to some good old-fashioned water management. Aerial photography can show up where old water courses ran in the past and these, once they cleaned out, become vast linear reservoirs that slow down the movement of water in very wet periods of weather, allowing rivers to cope better and so not to flood communities and farms further downstream. We must remember that once we start to interfere with and manage the natural world, we must continue with it or reap the consequences. Additional tree planting on upland areas of Yorkshire is now going on to help slow down water movement from moorlands. Perhaps the recently announced Northern Forest, running from Liverpool in the west to Hull in the east might also help to temper the effects of more and more extreme and sudden rainfall.

Height above sea level - if you can remember your Geography lessons at school, you may remember that for every 100 metres that you rise up above sea-level, the temperature will drop, on average, by 1°C. At just under 200 metres above sea level, I can expect my garden to be an average 2°C cooler than the beach at Scarborough. However, here on the outskirts of Huddersfield, in the rain shadow of the Pennines, other factors also influence the temperature - namely, cloud cover, cooling rain and wind.

SEASONS AND SEASONAL CHANGES

The 2009–2010, 2010–2011, 2012–2013 and 2017–2018 winters hopefully finally made us all realise that the Yorkshire garden can never be sub-tropical, despite the best efforts of successive TV gardeners, garden magazines, garden centres and other influences in our lives since the beginning of the 1980s. We were encouraged to plant a continually increasing list of sub-tropical, drought resistant and warm temperate plants in our gardens, including Antipodean Cordylines, Callistemons and Dicksonia tree ferns, Arabian and Asian palms, Mediterranean Olives and many, many more. During the spring and early summer of 2011, many of these died as a result of the coldest period of weather in December 2010 and January 2011 for 100 years. This period of weather was devastating for commercial growers as well as amateur gardeners and yet, as soon as the garden centres and DIY outlets presented us with the 2011 summer bedding plants in early April, amateur gardeners rushed like Lemmings to buy them, forgetting that frosts can kill plants in one night in April and May, let alone the 3-4 weeks of deep, penetrating frosts of winter. There is a season for every plant - accept it and do not try to cheat unless you have the facilities to do so - a heated glasshouse and a cold frame allows the gardener to 'harden off' tender bedding plants in readiness for the end of May when summer bedding plants and half-hardy vegetables can go out into warm soil and warm nights without any fear of being damaged by an unsuitable climate.

In the spring of 2012, after a sub-tropical late March and fears of a drought in certain parts of the UK, let alone a hose pipe ban, heavy and persistent rain from mid April filled every reservoir and underground aquifer, with farmers and growers complaining about the amount of rainfall instead of the lack of it - the wettest summer for 100 years with a long range forecast of similar summers to come. This summer also produced the longest and largest ice melt in the Arctic Circle recorded since satellite imaging began in the 1960s. The excessive rainfall continued, unabated, throughout the autumn period causing more flooding across large areas of the UK. By the end of 2012, we had had one of the wettest years ever! The winter of 2013–14 gave us another deluge and put thousands of acres of productive land under water, let alone putting thousands of us out of house, home and business for up to three months.

One of the strangest winters that many of us have ever experienced must be the 2017–2018 winter. For many of us, four periods of snow, two 'beasts from the East' and an unprecedented number of frosts put the spring back by as much as 4 weeks, delaying emergence of herbaceous plants, sowing and planting times and causing physiological damage to many of our precious garden plants, let alone causing the nesting season to be delayed and the arrival of migratory birds to be delayed and even stopped altogether! This period of winter weather was then followed by nearly three months of warm, sunny weather that allowed our gardens and the wider natural world to catch up. Spectacular displays of flowers on many of our native and cultivated trees and shrubs showed themselves. Drought conditions reminiscent of the 1976 summer followed in May, June and July, causing even more confusion to our plants and wildlife.

I will make no further attempts to discuss the larger issues of global warming and climate change as they have been alternatively described. Suffice it to say that we will, almost certainly, reap what we have sown, if we are not already doing so!

TOPOGRAPHY AND GEOLOGY OF YORKSHIRE

Being the countries largest county, albeit divided in to a number of distinct political areas, you can imagine that its topography and geology are incredibly varied.

Without too much mental strain, those of us that live in Yorkshire will be aware of the Limestone pavements of the Yorkshire Dales and the vast *Calluna vulgaris* (Ling Heather) moorlands of the North York Moors, the northern edges of the Peak District National Park and the lowland peat bogs of South Yorkshire. You may be aware of the sandy loams of the Vale of York that allowed people in Pontefract to grow the very deep-rooted plant *Glycyrrhiza glabra* (Liquorice) and Easingwold to be known as the ant capital of Yorkshire (ground living ants prefer the softer, drier soils based on sands). These, and many other variations in bed rock and soil types, have a major influence on what we can grow, from extremes of acidity to extremes of alkalinity as well as the ease of soil cultivation, from soft, sandy loams to unstable alluvial silts to almost impossible to manage heavy clays.

Add to these the almost infinite variations in the topography of our landscape and you cannot imagine a more varied but fascinating place to grow plants.

Height above sea level can vary from 1 metre in the lowest part of the Vale of York to 736 metres on the top of Whernside in North Yorkshire – the highest place in all of Yorkshire. The undulating landscape creates all sorts of opportunities and problems for gardens, from North facing slopes that never see the sun from October to February to South facing slopes that provide early planting opportunities for farmers and growers.

These topographical and geological variations must be one of the first considerations for anyone moving to a Yorkshire property. The study of your local geology via the Internet or a reference book in your local library might be a starting point but one of the best ways to help you understand what your house and garden are sitting on is to dig a 'soil profile pit.' Traditionally this would be a pit dug as a one cubic metre, showing you, as you delve deeper into the soil and bed rock, the depth of your top soil, the depth of your sub soil and the type of bed rock that they are formed from. During this process, you will be able to determine whether your soil is sandy, silty, clayey or of an organic nature, whether there is good, bad or indifferent drainage and finally, what the bed rock of your soil is – sandstone, millstone grit, limestone, shale or one of many other variants that Yorkshire has to offer. With a simple pH kit and a little observation of gardens and plants in your local area, you will be able to determine where your soil sits on the pH scale. Extreme alkalinity if you live in one of the many limestone pockets across the county or extreme acidity if you live near one of the acid moorlands, whether lowland near ones in South Yorkshire or the higher North Yorkshire moors. See Chapter 7 for more on the soil story.

CONCLUSION

I have often used an old statement to help gardeners cope with the peculiarities of their gardens – 'don't fight it, enjoy it.' In other words, if you have a free draining, sandy soil, grow plants that suit it. Do not try to grow too many moisture-loving plants unless you can create your own bog garden or pond. If you want to grow questionably tender plants, use or create a sheltered south facing wall that will retain heat at night and give full sun during the day. It all sounds very simple but requires us as organic gardeners to analyse the microclimates of our gardens, both above and below the surface, and use them to our plants' advantage, not ours!

The very light, sandy soils of the area around Selby are easily cultivated but are very easily eroded. Historically excellent for growing Glycyrrhiza glabra (Liquorice) in the Pontefract area.

The spectacular scenery of limestone escarpments and drystone walls of Littondale, within casting distance of Malham Cove and Malham Tarn. No Rhododendrons here but the remnants of old-fashioned hay meadows with their wonderful wild flowers !

Chapter Four

How to Manage your Plants and Gardens

There is a psychological distinction between cutting back and pruning. Pruning is supposed to be for the welfare of the tree or shrub; cutting back is for the satisfaction of the cutter.

Christopher Lloyd (1921–2006)
From: The Well-tempered garden (1973)

OVER THE 50+ years of gardening and perhaps more importantly, the 30+ years of teaching and training that I have had, I have watched hundreds of people, paid by local authorities and landscape companies carrying out what I can only describe as butchery to thousands of shrubs and trees, without giving any thought as to whether the technique or timing of the operation is going to benefit the plant or the landscape picture, let alone any wildlife that might want to benefit from flowers or fruit that the plant had been trying to produce.

Whether these 'pruning' operations have been forced upon the horticultural industry by bad design, incorrect plant choice or minimal or poor training, is impossible to tell but, one thing is certain – members of the public have taken the ideas and techniques to their hearts, adopting the hedgetrimmer as the preferred instrument of torture for unsuspecting shrubs and in fact any plant in the garden that dares to try and escape from its allotted space. Cast your eyes over the average garden wall and you will see these techniques repeated as shrub after shrub is manicured into a tight ball and trees are pruned back into objects that resemble Victorian hat stands. When you can watch someone, whose signage on their van suggests that they are 'Landscape Gardener', slaughtering an *Escallonia* hedge just as it comes into flower, you have to wonder why we call ourselves a 'nation of gardeners.' Perhaps a nation of garden owners might be a more accurate description!

Like all forms of gardening, the timing and techniques of pruning are all based on good observation, allowing the natural gardener to build up an image of what the plant does, when it does it and, most important of all, on what type of wood it does it on. If you study lists of shrubs and their basic pruning requirements, 50% of them need no regular pruning at all, although restoration pruning every 10 – 50 years may be needed with some. Visit Thorp Perrow Arboretum near Bedale in North Yorkshire and see a *Pieris formosa*, often seen as a small shrub for acidic soils, that has reached 5 metres in height after 60-70 years and hardly any pruning – by the way, it performs magnificently in spring and is loved by bees.

So, the big question is whether we should lock away the folding pruning saw, bypass secateurs, and the extendable loppers for good or just unlock them on selected occasions? Sorry, I forgot the hedgetrimmer - keep that locked up for the purpose of trimming hedges – the clue is in the name!

Traditionally, plants have been placed in their pruning groups according to the time of year that they require treatment alongside the specific technique required to make them perform at their best.

To take an obvious example that we all know. The spring flowering wall-shrub *Jasminum nudiflorum* (Winter Jasmine) normally finishes flowering by the end of March across most of Britain and it is at this stage, given the full length of the growing season ahead, that we can, if we feel it is necessary, take our secateurs out of the shed and remove about 10-20% of the plant, concentrating our efforts on older wood, dead wood, badly positioned wood and branches that have not flowered to their best. These actions will encourage the plant to replace the older growth with some stronger young shoots that will flower for us in two years time – a cyclical process that can go on, with various levels of intensity, for 50 years and more.

This quite specific technique is mirrored across the whole range of trees and shrubs that we choose to enhance our gardens – every plant has its own technique and timing to suit it and, although we might amend it to fit with our own gardens, the basic techniques do not alter.

Below I have listed some of the more commonly used techniques to help you find your way through the maze of ideas, with examples of plants that are suited to them but, to gain a fully understanding of techniques suited to

Jasminum nudiflorum immediately after pruning in April and three months later in July, producing lots of new growth in readiness for flowering again from September onwards – on a north facing wall!

individual species you will need to treat yourself or your hedgetrimmer happy partner to the RHS Pruning and Training book (see Bibliography for details) and try out the secateurs and pruning saw, watching the affects of your work over the following years to gauge whether you have been too brutal or too gentle. Remember that these techniques apply to fruit trees and bushes as well as ornamental ones, thus helping you to make your garden more productive as well as more beautiful. Correct pruning will also help to ensure that flowering plants produce their flowers in larger quantities, giving you the chance to support the pollinating and beneficial insects as well as them having a good chance of helping you.

Coppicing – an ancient pastime, traditionally used to produce building and fencing material and, as we come closer to modern times, wood for charcoal production. This means cutting back woodland trees such as *Castanea* (Sweet Chestnut), *Corylus* (Hazel), *Quercus* (Oak) and *Salix* (Willow) once every three to ten years depending upon the usage and the size of timber needed. Each main stem is cut back to within 15 - 30cm of its point of origin during the dormant season thus encouraging the tree to regenerate during the following

A group of Cordon grown Pyrus domestica (Pears) trained on a wall at a 45°angle.

growing season and beyond. It is still used today but more often as a way of encouraging environmental diversity within woodlands, although there are thankfully still a number of country craftsmen and women who use coppiced timber for building, furniture, baskets, fencing etc. The technique can be used for garden shrubs and trees. See stooling below.

Cordon, Espalier and Fan training - these, and many more techniques besides, have been developed over the centuries to control fruit and ornamental trees and shrubs in the garden, long before we had dwarfing and semi-dwarfing rootstocks to graft cultivars onto. Nowadays, with smaller spaces for us to garden in, these techniques are allowing us to grow trees against fences and walls to maximise the increasingly limited garden space that we have allotted to us.

Crown lifting, thinning and reduction - these processes go on without our interference in natural woodlands as lack of light in the crowns of trees causes some branches to die off. In our gardens this natural cycle does not occur as much and it requires us to intervene with our box of pruning tools to give nature a helping hand. The removal of unwanted lower branches that get in the way of lawns, paths, washing lines, buildings and sight lines should be a careful and gradual process from the day the tree is planted, only removing when absolutely necessary and always during the dormant season. Thinning out of congested and crossing branches in the crown of the tree should be done carefully and only when absolutely necessary to avoid stimulating further excessive or badly positioned growth elsewhere in the tree. Crown reduction is the decreasing of the overall dimensions of the crown and can be done without anyone knowing that the process has been undertaken. However, we have all seen examples of trees that look more like giant Victorian hat stands, leaving the tree never quite looking the same again. That is not pruning and should be condemned as wholesale butchery. Severe pruning only encourages excessive vegetative growth, to the detriment of flowering growth – not a good thing for organic gardeners as they try to support as much wildlife as possible.

For the pruning of larger, semi-mature and mature specimen trees it is advisable to search out the services of a good tree surgeon, perhaps starting with your local authority's Planning Department where they will have a list of recommended companies. Always check that they have current public liability insurance and also check with your Local Authority Planning Department whether the trees are covered by the various constraints of Tree Preservation Orders (TPO's), Conservation Area Orders (CAO's), Areas of Outstanding Natural Beauty (AONB's) or Sites of Special Scientific Interest (SSSI's) before you take any direct action.

Dead, diseased and damaged wood – walk past any piece of public or private landscape planting these days and you will find that the dead, diseased and damaged wood is created, not by the ravages of time but by the hedge trimmers that are used by private contractors and public servants alike, without a thought as to the visual impact, let alone any hidden costs and environmental impact – shrubs pruned to within a centimetre of their lives, lest they grow out of their allotted space - this is of course one of the main causes – they are planted far too close and so their allotted space is nowhere near as much as we might give them in a domestic environment. Thankfully, in our own gardens, we should have the time for and the emotional attachment to our shrubs and trees to ensure that we do not create problems but try to prevent the three d's or remove them if they occur naturally. Correct spacing of plants is one way of helping to prevent the occurrence of the three d's, followed by good aftercare. Only prune when absolutely necessary and when you do, follow the rules for the individual plant, let alone following the basic rules of pruning:- 1. Use clean, sharp tools. 2. Choose correct timing. 3. Remove leading shoots back to appropriately positioned laterals when reducing height and width of shrub or tree. 4. Remove laterals back to their point of origin rather than leaving

The before and after of selective thinning with a Ribes nigrum (Blackcurrant) after fruit has been harvested. Old, fruited branches are removed to leave space and energy for the new, stronger shoots to carry on growing. These then produce the best flowers and fruits for the following year.

short 'pegs' unless you are spur pruning. 5. For spur pruning, always cut the laterals back to a well-positioned and healthy looking bud. 6. When removing the three d's, do not shred and compost diseased material.

Selective thinning – one of the most effective methods for extending the life of a shrub and for stimulating new growth. Always best done on your hands and knees, this pruning technique involves the removal of 25% or more of the older stems and these are easier to recognise at ground-level because their bases are often thicker, darker and dirtier than their younger siblings. The action causes a minor and temporary imbalance in the relationship between the top growth and root system. With 100% roots and 75% top growth, the spring surge of sap flow will force some new wood to be produced – the only problem is that you will not necessarily be able to control where it appears from.

Spur pruning – a very effective method for fruit trees and shrubs that are trained onto walls, wires or other support systems. It involves the cutting back of annual lateral growth to 3-4 buds, usually towards the end of the growing season (August / September). This action allows light and air into ripening fruit and allows the plant to push its remaining sap and manufactured sugars and starches from photosynthesis into the ripening fruit. For flowering subjects the technique can help to stimulate the production of more flower buds and, overall, it helps to control the plant's spread upwards and outwards.

Stooling – the technique is, to all intents and purposes, the same as coppicing but can be practiced annually on shrubs such as *Cornus alba* (Dogwoods) and *Salix alba* (White Willows) to stimulate vigorous annual growth that has stronger bark colour. There is no need to cut the plants back to ground level and for *Buddleia* (Butterfly bush), *Eucalyptus* and *Sambucus* (Elderberry) for example it is advisable not to.

Salix alba vitellina 'Yelverton' (white willow) in the winter borders at RHS Gardens Harlow Carr prior to being stooled in spring to encourage vigorous summer growth.

Once you have mastered the various arts that make up good pruning, you must then ensure that you do not make bad choices of plants that force you into practising those newly acquired skills too often. This means ensuring that you choose the right plants for the right locations within your garden, using your now advanced plant knowledge and that, in the event of your pruning skills, plant knowledge or plant choice letting you down, you will be prepared to allow evolution to deal with the problem and use a sharp spade to remove the offending plant(s), thus giving you space to fill with a better selection of plants. I, like many garden owners, have succumbed to the problem of emotional attachment to plants. We all have at least one - those plants given to us by friends, relatives or neighbours that we feel must still have a space in our gardens, despite the fact that we may not even like the plant or that it has grown out of all proportion to its originally allotted spaced. Start by taking a cutting or some seed to ensure that

The heather bed at the RHS Gardens Harlow Carr near Harrogate. On this scale they are a winter wonder and are much sort after by Queen Bumble Bees. Maybe we should all start planting them again.

you do not lose the plant altogether - do not throw out the parent plant until its offspring have been given the chance to survive. Once this has been guaranteed, the original gift can be discarded without fear of reprisals from visiting friends, relatives or neighbours.

Read on for more ideas on how to make good choices and how to encourage your garden to evolve over time.

Plant choice - how do we make our choices? The media has, in all its strange guises over recent years, had a worrying influence on us, tempting us to buy plants that naturally we might not if we were not exposed to glittering images on the television and in magazines. In the 1990s we were being tempted with drought resistant and sub-tropical plants because that was where it had been perceived our climate was moving to. Conifers and heathers were all the rage in the 1970s and alpines and roses had their heyday in the 1950s and 1960s. With our ever more extreme climate in recent years, it might be wise to stick to the wide diversity of plants that have been grown and known over the last 100 years or more, rather than choosing the latest 'must have' plants that a television celebrity tells us is the latest fashion accessory.

Plant knowledge – one of the things that 50 + years in the industry has taught me is how little I know! With several tens of thousands of plants still to learn, I am unlikely to acquire knowledge of all of them before I cast off my mortal toil. However, as every day goes past, I usually learn one or more new facts or plant names and it is this that drives me and every other gardener and horticulturist on. When you come across a new plant, try not to learn just its name. Ask yourself the following 10 questions and then use good reference books and the internet to resolve them:

1. When does it flower and fruit?

2. What type of plant material does it flower on? – young growth, mature growth, short spurs etc.

3. How and when does the plant need pruning or cutting back?

4. What are its soil requirements? – acid, alkaline, heavy, light, well-drained, wet, warm, cold.

5. What type of climatic conditions does it need? – tropical, temperate, sunny, shady etc.

6. How can it be propagated and when?

7. Does any part of it have any medicinal, aromatic or culinary value and is any part of it an irritant or poisonous?

8. Does it have any specific pests or diseases associated with it?

9. Where does the plant originate from and how does that relate to cultivating it?

10. Lastly, but by no means least, what value does the plant have for wildlife as a place to feed, breed or shelter?

These ten questions will provide answers that, in themselves, will raise more questions. See the bibliography for examples of worthy reference books that may provide some of the answers to the questions posed above.

Garden evolution – removing one or two offending monstrous plants from the garden is, for some of us, an accepted norm. Redesigning a whole new border to replace one that you have become wholly sick and tired of is in a different league. Most of us, with our allotted domestic garden space do not get involved with gardening until we are in our mid to late twenties at the earliest. Taking a normal life span until we are in our eighties, by which time energy levels, eyesight and agility will probably have cut our gardening days shorter if not completely, this gives us around 50 to 60 years of gardening to enjoy. During that time our life style, commitments, responsibilities, financial well-being, physical well-being and many other factors will have changed many times and, as they do, our views on the priorities for that little piece of planet earth will change accordingly.

These subtle changes in our lives, that might also include moving house a few times, mean that our gardens change in tune with our lives. It is because of these subtle, sometimes almost unseen changes, that we must be prepared to encourage our garden to evolve in the same way as the insides of our domestic properties evolve. Carpets, flooring, curtains, furniture and wall coverings are always on our interior decoration agenda these days and so it must be in the garden.

Lawns – do you really need all those vast sweeping hectares of grass that serve little other purpose than somewhere to kick a ball or occupy the man of the house with his mower on a Sunday morning? Lawns are a British concept that are in no way productive and serve very little purpose for wildlife, other than a place to scatter bird seed in winter and for blackbirds and starlings to search for worms and insect grubs. They act as a green background to beds and borders in much the same way as a carpet does in the lounge – look where the carpet has gone in recent years! It has been replaced by wooden flooring – less time consuming and better for people with dust allergies – by the way, I am not advocating the newest fad to hit the unwary gardener, whether organic or otherwise – the artificial lawn!. Evolve your lawn by gradually reducing it and planting some more fruit, vegetables or ornamental plants. Add another small patio to give you an extra outdoor seating area in the sun or shade to allow you to sit and observe or just to sit. With less lawn to cut you will have more time to sit and enjoy your garden and there will be a lot less neighbourhood noise to disturb the wildlife and your neighbours.

Fruit and vegetable gardens – the latest trend in our society is to have allotments, community gardens, even 'incredible edibles' in our high streets (started by two ladies from Todmorden) to help us lead a healthier life style – exercising when we are producing them and eating healthily when we get the produce into the kitchen. The trend within our own allotted garden space is now to have pots of herbs on the patio, fruit trees and bushes in the borders and vegetables in raised beds to ease of access and production. If we look back to the days of the cottage garden, used by our forebears in rural environments, before we all moved to towns and cities in the early part of the 19th century, they practiced a fully mixed garden where flowers, fruit, herbs and vegetables all grew in chaotic harmony – this makes better use of garden space and gets us away from the rigidity of traditional gardening techniques such as monoculture, wide spacings and strict sowing and planting times. Whichever path you choose, your own garden will surely be more productive and valuable.

Flower borders – throw away the rule book and allow flowers to search out their own space in your garden – test out their preferences for light and shade, wet and dry in your garden by planting the same plant in three or four different locations and see how they perform – you may be surprised. However, to be able to do this you will need more space for planting. See lawns, above, for a possible solution. Test out wild flowers in the garden but stop sprinkling an annual dose of fertiliser as they will not like it. Try out some hardy annuals that can be sown directly into the garden in autumn or spring rather than expensive spring and summer bedding that need a lot of watering, feeding and dead-heading to make them perform to their best. If some of your herbaceous plants

A cottage garden mix of hardy annuals is so easy to care for. Corn marigolds and ox-eye daisies will self-seed and need little attention other than removal at the end of summer.

such as *Delphiniums, Heucheras, Hostas* and *Liliums* are constantly plagued by foreign pests, stop growing them! If you want more wildlife to frequent your garden, look out for plants that can provide a food source of pollen, nectar, seeds or fruits and compost a few of those that do not provide these necessary things.

Patios – these apparently unproductive areas of our gardens are often just part of an access route from one part of the garden to another. You need to ask yourself and your family how you use the garden and whether, as your life evolves, you need a quiet patio in the shade to allow you a spot for reading or an afternoon cuppa. Do you like sun bathing? If so, build a patio facing south or south west. Have you developed a liking for herbs for culinary use? If so, a sunny patio is the best place for them. Either planted into notches between the slabs or in pots on the slabs.

Outbuildings – with 'National Shed Week' now a regular feature in the nation's calendar, we should consider anything on our property that is broadly an outbuilding as a potentially valuable gardening place or space. As our lives evolve, the man of the house might fancy turning all or part of the shed / garage into his 'office', now retitled the 'Shoffice'. The lady of the house may consider a 'summer house' to be an essential addition to the garden where she can escape the clatter of his poorly advanced keyboard skills in his office. The garden shed of course is an essential for gardeners to store all the accoutrements needed to follow this ancient art – wheelbarrows, labels, pots, hand tools, garden canes, a ball of twine, fertilizers, seed sowing and potting compost, seed trays – the list goes on. See Chapter 10 for more on garden tools and gadgets.

Glasshouses – a fabulous addition to any property as the enthusiasm for gardening increases and a wonderful opportunity to extend the growing season for a wider and more diverse range of plants presents itself. Of course, for the word glasshouse, also read cold frames, polythene tunnels, cloches and bell jars as they are all there to extend the growing season and to protect, temporarily or permanently, any plant that is not originally from our Northern temperate climate. Sadly we can see many gardens where a glasshouse has been erected in a moment of enthusiasm by the owner or tenant, only to become neglected when it is realised how much time and effort is required to make a success of it. When you are away on your holidays, have you got a willing neighbour or friend who is able to care for your plants?

Boundary hedges and fences – both of these are discussed elsewhere in the book but, both features have a habit of evolving without us even noticing.

Hedges tend to grow in height and width, despite our best efforts with the hedgetrimmer once or twice a year, and there will come a time when drastic action is needed to prevent half your garden disappearing behind a wall of shade or a widening hedge. At this point it is sometimes best to have a clean slate and start all over again. With mixed, wildlife friendly hedges, they will usually respond to a severe pruning or even hedge laying if you have the skills or the money to buy those skills in.

Fences are a mixed blessing, giving us instant privacy but requiring rather more maintenance that we might have thought. Painting and repairs are routine tasks if you want the fence to last more than eight or nine years. Many modern fences seal the garden in from the surrounding landscape and prevent our wild animals from being able to roam free in search of food and a mate. Try to have at least one boundary open to the outside world, where at all possible or at least cut a hedgehog sized hole in the base of your fence panels to allow them to wander freely.

Conclusions

Of all the thinking that can and does go on about the garden, it is the longer-term management that seems to pass us by. Whether it unruly shrubs and trees, changing lifestyles or the allocation of priorities of time and money that stop us from the getting the best out of our 'little piece of Yorkshire', we all need to sit back and think about our gardens with the same amount of effort and dedication as we do with the indoor parts of our properties. Scribble your list of do's and don'ts below, when you have the time!

Chapter Five

Capability Brown, Eat Your Heart Out!

He therefore who would see his flower's disposed
Sightly in a just order, 'ere he gives
The beds the trusted treasure of their seeds
Forecasts the future whole, that when the scene
Shall break into its preconceived display,
Each for itself, and all as with one voice
Conspiring, may attest his bright design.

William Cowper (1731–1800)
From: The Task Book iii – The Garden (1785)

GARDEN DESIGN IDEAS have changed as often over the millennia as have styles of houses, shoes, dresses and many other aspects of our lives. In fact these are some of the indicators of the health and wealth of a nation. I wonder, when future generations look back on us, how they will see the gardens of the late 20th and early 21st Centuries? At the beginning of the 20th Century Gertrude Jekyll was praised for her designs and planting ideas and yet William Robinson was not! At the end of the 20th Century, Alan Titchmarsh was praised for his garden designs that formed part of the garden make-over series Ground Force and yet, Diarmuid Gavin's designs for show gardens at RHS Chelsea Flower Show were frowned upon by many as he tried to push the boundaries of garden design occasionally a little too far!

The range of plants, building materials and ideas has never been greater and yet, cast your eyes over the garden wall and in many gardens you will still see random chaos. Is this because British people are by definition reactive rather than proactive in their adoption of new ideas? The mad rush to acquire decking, tree ferns, blue painted timber and gravel in the 1990s and very early 21st Century have now burnt themselves out and everyone is now waiting for another new idea to pop out of an RHS Chelsea Flower Show garden or off the television screens - naturalistic gardens, with wild flowers and the cottage garden effects seem to be the flavour of the decade – William Robinson advocated these ideas 100 years ago in his wonderful book, 'The English Flower Garden', and was not very popular as the last pangs of the strict formality of the Victorian era were fading – is this another case of history repeating itself?

And yet, when you study the essential elements of a garden, most small to medium sized domestic gardens will almost design themselves.

Consider the following 10 essentials of urban and suburban living, let alone rural living, which the vast majority of us have chosen to live in. They determine their own position and space allocation for the large majority of British garden owners.

1. A place for wheelie-bins – both general rubbish and recycling bins and other assorted containers provided by our local authorities.

2. A place to dry the washing outdoors - more environmentally friendly than a tumble dryer or the central heating radiator in the spare bedroom and a lot cheaper.

3. A place for the compost heap(s) – an absolute must in all modern environmentally friendly gardens.

4. A place to sit in the sun (patio).

5. A place to sit in the shade (patio or summer house).

6. At least three manhole covers (in my own garden I have five)! Sorry – sewage access chambers if you want to be politically correct!!

7. Access paths around the house and to some or all of the essential things highlighted above.

8. Boundary fences / hedges not owned by you.

9. Boundary fences / hedges owned by you.

10. A garden shed or other outbuilding that needs to be easily accessible.

Not much left of the typical small suburban garden now to carry out all these fancy designs, is there?

Of course, some of these essentials can be combined together and some may not actually be essential for you but, if you ever watched any of the garden make-over programmes of the 1990s and again in the 2010s, you will realise that few if any of these things were ever considered, or even mentioned, in the pretty, airy-fairy designs that are apparently slung together in a few short days!

Continuity is one aspect of garden design and construction that frustrates me. I live in a sandstone / millstone grit area of West Yorkshire, surrounded by drystone walls and stone built houses and yet, walk up the average street in the village and you will see limestone rockeries, red brick paths and walls, blue painted fencing and other timber constructions, timber path edges, red gravel and many other materials that have little to do with this area of the country and they grate on the senses, at least for me! Historically people did not travel too far away from their own homes and so any materials used indoor or out were sourced locally or regionally. Nowadays, we can buy from anywhere on the planet and within a few short days it arrives on the back of a lorry or inside an unmarked white van!

Lifestyle – our properties will always reflect the people that live in them and usually our gardens demonstrate who we are. A less active family will have few trees, shrubs and herbaceous plants because of the apparent need for regular physical excursion and are likely to have a 'lawn' and fencing that are apparently easy to care for – even an artificial lawn! A keen gardener will often have an eclectic mix of plants because their enthusiasm for plants steers them towards nurseries, gardens and garden centres where there are lots of plants for sale – when they arrive home, they find a space to put their new purchases – an eclectic mix evolves, with randomly placed plants in randomly shaped and placed borders and beds. A young family usually does not have the time to work a garden fully and so limits itself to a simple outdoor space for play and healthy exercise until the children move on. Some families include the garden space as a natural part of family life, with fruit and vegetables being a part of that lifestyle, and they even extend into an allotment to fulfil their desire for fresh fruit and vegetables, if not pretty flowers. Does your garden reflect your personality?

Love of gardening – this strange thing that can take over peoples' lives often comes from previous generations. For my part, I was encouraged by a distant relative that we lived with when I was a child – she had been a florist and loved her garden. I was given a small patch to care for at the age of 8 and, as they say in all the good books, never looked back. This love of the activities and processes of gardening helps you to place plants and features in the most suitable position in the garden to get the very best performance out of them, and thus, this influences the overall design of your garden.

Allotted space – in my experience of viewing gardens from a judge's viewpoint, let alone from a personal perspective, it is not the size of the garden that makes a good garden but the gardener. The same is also true of the size of the bank balance – it is not how much you spend but whether you spend it wisely.

Desire to show off to your neighbours – keeping up with the Jones's is one of my pet hates and, in the world of garden design, this rather odd British desire to have something that someone else has got is not what an organic gardener should be considering. Walk slowly down any urban or suburban street and you will see the copycat mentality so typical of us British. The best gardens are the ones that truly reflect the owners and not their neighbours.

Need for privacy – I have never understood this phenomenon but it is worthy of a few short moments of time to discuss it. In semi-detached suburbia you are very unlikely to have the opportunity to sun bathe naked in the garden as you will be overlooked by at least two properties at any one time so why do you need privacy? In these days of community involvement, our gardens should give us a link to our neighbours, not separate us from them. So, if you feel that you need privacy in your life, buy a house at least one kilometre from any other, surround yourself and your family with evergreen trees and hedges and become a hermit. If the sun does shine, make sure that you use plenty of Factor 50 on those sensitive bits!

Principles of design – I have set out a few ideas for you to follow when you have the unenviable task of designing your garden, particularly if it is your first time.

1. When moving into a new house that has been lived in previously, apart from routine maintenance, leave the garden to show itself to you for at least twelve months so that you can gauge the performance of the established plants, the soil and the micro-climates as well as deciding on what you love and what you hate. You may also find those unwanted 'weeds' in amongst the more cultivated plants.

2. Draw, or have drawn for you, a basic scale plan of the garden and house and make a number of copies on tracing paper. On one you can write

A generic view across the bottom of my garden, where wildlife and flowers sit happily together, whilst I sit happily together with my wife and family watching the antics of birds, butterflies and other wild visitors and residents enjoying the tranquillity that I have attempted to create and care for.

in boundary ownerships and responsibilities and you can indicate any neighbours and their gardens, with any associated issues that may impact on your garden such as trees, hedges and shade. You can also include any existing outbuildings that you do not intend to demolish or relocate. On another you can indicate any topographical, geographic and geological issues that may influence path layouts, patios, retaining walls, lawns, frost pockets and drainage and other water related issues. On another you can draw in manholes, sewers, overhead services, television and internet cables, as these may limit any excavations and proposed trees. If you now overlay each of these, you will see a picture emerging that will either influence the placing of certain features or will determine their position for you. Humphrey Repton used a similar technique in his 'Red Book's' during his working life as a Landscape Designer during the late 18th and early 19th centuries.

3. Wish lists are always another good starting point to any garden design, giving you and your family an idea of what you might want in the garden over the next 10 years or so. As each of these usually has a rather specific

Not for the small domestic garden but we can all dream. Start putting those well-earned pennies away in a piggy bank!

requirement for orientation, sunlight levels, and location in relation to the house, these can be added to one of your draft plans as simple templates (drawn to the same scale as the master plan) so that you can move them around until you are happy with their position. The features that you might write on your list include: Sunny patio, shady patio, compost heap(s), glasshouse, sheds and other outbuildings, cold frame, vegetable garden, fruit garden, washing lines, access paths, recycling and other domestic waste bin containers, ponds or other water features and of course, existing garden features that you want to remove or restore. If you are considering any extensions to the property or alternations to the footprint of the building(s) these will need to be included in this equation.

4. As gardens are, by definition, based on soil, it is advisable to dig a soil pit (1 cubic metre) so that you can assess the top soil and its texture and structure, the subsoil and its influence on drainage and water tables and, if you can dig that far down, the bed rock that influences your soil pH and fertility. You might carry this out as part of excavations for a pond. During this process you can take a number of top soil samples and measure the pH as well as Nitrogen, Phosphorous and Potassium levels. To help you to advance your understanding of your garden and its soil, you might also take a gentle stroll

This stunning lake can be found at The Himalayan Gardens near Grewelthorpe in North Yorkshire but, I wonder what they found out about their soil type when they dug that out?

around your estate to see what others have done and what plants they are growing – this is not 'keeping up with the Jones's' but learning from them.

5. Size is everything, or so we're told. Well, over the last 30 years or so garden sizes in new-build estates have shrunk to an all-time low and it is essential that, for those of us with these new mini-gardens, we learn from Dr Who and turn our gardens into a Tardis (Time and relative dimension in space). Not literally, but, with careful design, we can put a lot more into our gardens than we might think. Ideas such a building garden seating that has lockable storage underneath reduces the need for a garden shed; using multi-layered planting to get as much into each square metre as we can; using paved areas for planting low growing herbs; using any vertical space to grow climbers and fruit trees against and using shrubs and trees as climbing frames for climbing plants are just a few ideas to get you thinking about maximising each square metre.

6. Once individual beds and borders have been given a place, a size and a shape, you have the complex but fascinating task of designing a planting plan. This might be a crop rotation plan for a vegetable garden or a planting plan for a new ornamental border. The rules of colour combinations and height are very complex and, when you read Christopher Lloyd's books

The winding paths through the winter borders at RHS Gardens Harlow Carr allow us to see that, when plants are used in decent numbers, the impact is much more powerful that it might be with just one or two. Think big. Think bold.

or watch any of his televised pieces, it makes you realise that the rules are made to be broken, tested and re-written. In ornamental borders, you should try to ensure that there is something performing in each week, let alone month, of the year, not just for your satisfaction but for the benefit of any wildlife that might wish to take advantage of it. This usually means using the multi-layered idea mentioned above – spring, summer, autumn and winter 'bulbs' to pop their heads up when you least expect it; climbers scrambling through larger shrubs and trees; herbaceous plants coming and going with each season; temporary spring and summer flushes of hardy annuals; shrubs providing flowers, foliage and fruits for you and your feathered or furry friends; fruit, vegetables and herbs to give the border some culinary value as well as its core ornamental one. All of these should suggest that the border(s) need to be a decent size to contain all these variations. For the most part, British domestic gardens have borders that are far to regimented and narrow, maximising the area of grass / lawn for you to take care of! Think big.

7.   Continuity is not something we seem to be very good as British gardeners and property owners. Is it because, as a race of people, we are reactive rather than proactive to new ideas, products and materials? When

it comes to the hard landscaping of our gardens, unless we have had a complete makeover by an expensive designer and associated landscaper, most of our gardens are a hotchpotch of different materials and colours that seldom fit with our houses or our local area. As new ideas emerge onto the market place, instead of saying 'that's a nice new colour, I must paint my fence with it,' we should be saying 'does it fit with my garden layout and the style of properties in the area?' The same is true of paving materials, containers, arches, outbuildings, pergolas, gazebos and seating.

8. Longevity – a tree is for life not just for Christmas – this should be a new slogan for our garden centre and nursery industry but, unfortunately, they seem to be more concerned about profit and tempting you back to spend more money as often as they can, with the result that we have been encouraged to buy transitory plants for little flashes of colour rather than plants that give us, and any associated wildlife, any longer term benefits – a diverse and complex ecosystem does not have time to develop on plants that only last from June to October!

9. Layers – ecological studies over recent years have identified a number of layers in natural woodlands that support different groups of creatures and, in order for us to be able to provide the same level of support to any permanent or transitory garden wildlife, our gardens must try to simulate those various layers. The first layer is the tree canopy that may be represented in a garden by trees or larger shrubs, giving a site for protection, breeding, shelter, viewing, feeding etc for any wildlife that chooses to pay a call. The second layer is the shrub layer that consists of larger and small shrubs and hedges, giving feeding, shelter, breeding sites for a wide diversity of organisms. The third layer is the herbaceous plants that consist of grasses and other soft herbaceous plants, including bulbs and this layer provides a feeding site for many organisms as well as a breeding site for some smaller creatures. The final layer is the woodland floor that is below ground as well as above and may include decomposers such as beneficial bacteria and fungi, beetles, woodlice etc.

This final part of the garden design chapter is, from my perspective, the most important because it allows you to gradually develop a garden that provides everything that you require as well as a little of what nature requires, giving both parties somewhere to be healthy and happy!

Chapter Six

The Good, The Bad and The Ugly Plants in The Garden

Flowers in my time which everyone would praise,
Though thrown like weeds from gardens nowadays.

John Clare (1793-1864)
From: The Cross Road; or, The Haymakers Story

IF THE SEEDS that we purposefully sow would germinate as well as the ones that blow in from a neighbour's garden, we would all have much more beautiful and productive gardens. This statement is reflected across the whole of the gardening world – a rhizomatous patch of ground elder will spread across the garden faster than you can dig it out but that new rhizomatous Iris that you wanted to complete a new border just does not want to grow!! Your newly sown row of carrots will often be drowned in chickweed and groundsel long before that thin green line of recognisable carrot seedlings have appeared. That, I am afraid is the price we pay for trying to manage the natural world rather than working with it.

If you take a walk around your local woods, fields and hedgerows, you will be able to see a range of plants that seem to thrive, without human intervention but without a 'weed' in sight. Stroll around your local area and you will see certain groups of plants that obviously like the soil and the climate. These two images, that can be built up easily when you move into a new area, will help you to avoid trying to grow plants that do not like the area and this will save you a lot of money, time and frustration.

BAD PLANTS

I am sure that we have all heard the old saying that 'One year's seeding is seven years weeding.' Not strictly true but a good indicator for an organic gardener that, if he / she allows a weed to set and distribute its bounty of seed, it is likely to cause annoyance for some time to come. Take over a previously neglected garden or allotment and, although you might be able to clear the surface debris and obvious weed growth in a relatively short time, the soil will be infested with roots, rhizomes, stolons, seeds, tap roots and tubers, to keep you occupied for many years to come. With ever increasing concerns about the use and impact of pesticides in our world, let alone the gradual reduction in their availability, we need to consider less harmful ways of ridding our gardens of these invaders, perhaps going back a few decades to the time to when physical weed control was the accepted norm because the chemical means were not available and yet the labour was.

The stale seed bed technique of weed control is one such idea that our forebears knew about and used to some effect when labour was cheap and

Weed such as Senecio jabobaea (Ragwort) will self-seed freely with their wind-distributed seed. It is poisonous to cattle and horses but supports the six-spot burnet moth and the cinnabar moth. The horns of a dilemma for those that want to support wildlife.

plentiful. Now that we have scores of variations on the title of herbicide that will, according to the adverts, clear our ground in an instant, it would seem that we no longer want or apparently need to spend time clearing the ground thoroughly before we attempt to grow a crop. The stale seed bed technique relies on a cycle of cultivation and re-growth that allows the weeds to grow from seed or some underground storage organ and then for these to be hoed, dug or, as a last resort, sprayed to stop their growth at an early stage and allow them to dry out before carrying out the same tasks again – this can be used on neglected allotments to very great effect over the first growing season or two so that by year three if it badly infested, the plot will be almost weed free, apart from wind-blown seed from other allotments or creeping rhizomes that wander under the boundary fence onto your allotted space! It can also be used on a fallow piece of ground if you are practicing a four or five year crop rotation, with the dead and dying weeds adding to the organic matter content of the soil.

This technique of weed control does not, of course, give you the rest of your gardening life free of those invasive plants that rob your cultivated plants of essential light, nutrients, space and water. Weed control, in its broadest sense, is a necessary part of the management of any garden environment. The 'weed' may be a rogue seedling from a nearby tree such as *Acer pseudoplatanus* (Sycamore) or *Fraxinus excelsior* (Ash) that have been blown or transported into your garden by other means. It may be one of the typical ephemeral, annual, biennial or perennial weeds that we all know and 'love.' It may be a rather invasive cultivated plant that you inherited or brought in to your garden, only to regret it a few weeks, months or years later. Whichever way these unwanted plants arrive in your garden, like most other plants, they will find their own space, soil and situation and it is for you to understand their peculiarities and use techniques of control that suit the situation, the weed and the 'crop' that occupies that part of the garden.

Over the last two hundred years or so since 'modern' gardening began to show itself, our plant hunters have brought back to our shores many delightful plants for us to cultivate, including *Persicaria* (syn. *Fallopia*) *japonica* (Japanese Knotweed), *Heracleum mantegazzianum* (Giant Hogweed), *Impatiens glandulifera* (Himalayan Balsam) and *Rhododendron ponticum* to name but a few land-based foreign invaders! The list of water-based invaders is just as long! See **Aquatics** below for a list.

Other ways of helping to reduce the problems created by our 'weeds' include:

1. **Checking newly purchased plants** – the top layer of compost in some container grown plants from nurseries and garden centres can be infested with invisible weed seeds – if you can, scrape the top 25mm of compost off and do not put it in on the compost heap – weeds such as *Cardamine hirsuta* (Hairy Bitter Cress) and *Salix caprea* (Goat Willow) will leap across your garden quicker than you can run with a hoe. Remove the plant from its pot to see if there are any other nasty surprises below soil level – the roots and rhizomes of invasive perennials that will run amuck across your garden once you have planted the new purchase or the ubiquitous vine weevil grubs.

2. **The early bird catches the worm** – or should that be the flowering weed! In our mixed borders weeds such as *Poa annua* (Annual Meadow Grass) and *Chamaenerion* (Syn.*Epilobium*) spps (Willowherbs) will produce thousands of seeds if we do not catch them early enough in their growing season – vigilance and a small garden fork or hoe is all that is required to stop your borders from being overrun by these weeds.

3. **Weaker weeds are easier to kill** – for some of our more invasive perennial weeds, the use of herbicides should be our last resort, not our first. Research that is emerging from one of our continental cousins has shown that weeds can actually develop resistance to certain herbicides, making them impossible to kill by chemical means. You have been warned!

    By constantly cutting off any top growth you can weaken the weeds before you choose to treat them with an appropriate chemical. Often spot weeding is sufficient rather than a blanket spray across the whole border. It may also be advisable to remove as many of your cultivated plants as you can before you treat the weeds to a dose of some vile herbicide. These plants will need to be checked for roots, stolons and rhizomes of any invasive weeds before you replant and you should read the instructions for the chemical to ensure that it will not leave any harmful residues in the soil for months afterwards.

4. **Growing conditions** – although we can recognise that certain weeds grow in particular garden situations, it is a lesser known fact that it is

Chamaenerion (Syn.Epilobium) angustifolium (Rosebay Willowherb) along with many other willowherbs, has wind-distributed seeds and a perennial root-system, causing them to pop up in our gardens without us even knowing. The Rosebay Willowherb supports the Elephant Hawk Moth – another dilemma!

the growing conditions that control whether weeds appear and not the fact that a certain weed will only grow on a vegetable plot or in a lawn. A wet lawn is more likely to grow a good crop of moss, coarse grasses and buttercups than a dry one. A rich soil is more likely to support a good crop of stinging nettles and docks than a poor one. A starved lawn will encourage field woodrush and yarrow where a healthy lawn will encourage plantains and dandelions.

See Appendix 3 for a list of weeds and suggested ways to help you rid your garden of each of them. When you read through the lists, look out for the foreign invaders that have tried to take over our gardens and countryside over the years.

Algae, lichen, liverworts and mosses – do we see these as 'weeds' in the broadest sense of the word?

Well, if you have ever skidded on a slippery patio, watched your pond turn into pea green soup in summer or cursed the latest patch of moss that has developed on your lawn, the answer will be a resounding 'yes.'

Walk through any ancient woodland and see bright orange lichen growing on a tree trunk, or walk slowly along the shady side of a drystone wall and observe the brilliant green of a cushion moss and the answer will be a definite 'no.'

Lichens, Liverworts and mosses are classified as Bryophytes from a botanical view point and can be found wherever the conditions are suitable – lawns, the surface of the compost in a pot and rotting tree trunks, to name but a few. Algae falls into a complex group that contains seaweeds, the blue-green algae of static water and the green, often slimy layer that we find on paving,

This Limestone drystone wall in Littondale is covered in moss encouraged by the shade of the Fraxinus excelsior (Ash) trees and the normally high rainfall of the area. Imagine being a nesting bird in search of a soft bed for your chicks!

fencing etc, absorbing Carbon dioxide and causing no harm to anything but us humans. Lichen is formed from a symbiotic relationship between a fungus and an algae or bacterium and can be found on your lawn and on the trunks of shrubs and trees in damp and shady places, not damaging them in any way. These apparently simple plants are amongst the oldest living organisms on the planet and are just as important to the development and maintenance of our garden ecology as all the other thousands of components, both seen and unseen.

GOOD PLANTS

The desire to propagate plants is instinctive for any good gardener and, in the gentle wanderings around the estate, he / she will be constantly on the lookout for a propagation opportunity, either because he / she wants more of that particular plant in the garden or because it will provide some spare stock for swapping with like-minded people.

I have grouped the plants for our gardens according to how they grow or where we might choose to grow them. Of course, this does not stop you from growing plants outside of their normally accepted slot in the garden, or for that matter, the plants choosing their own location according to their needs rather than yours.

Alpines – these tiny relatives of our larger garden plants have evolved to cope with three extremes – intense light, extremes of temperature and poor soil. Their flowering is often early in the growing season to give them the longest period possible for seed to develop and to germinate before the ravages of winter seal them in an icy overcoat for up to six months of the year – for us this means harvesting seed as soon as it is ripe and sowing it immediately under cold glasshouse protection. As many alpine plants live on scree slopes and rocky outcrops, their structure has adapted to manage the damage caused by stones crashing into their apparently delicate stems – the rosette formation of many alpines allows small pieces to be broken off, only for them to drop into a small crevice further down the slope and take root – a strong hint as to the propagation technique that we might try. Some of the 'alpines' that are sold these days are in fact plants from rocky maritime environments but, given high light and good drainage, these should form a good partnership with the true alpines.

Aquatic plants – not for everyone because some of us do not have a pond, although some will still have the smart bubble fountains and other 'aquatic' features from the era of television's Ground Force and similar programmes – most have no value as places for growing aquatic plants and even less have any value for visiting or residential wildlife. However, under this generic title of aquatic plants there is a list of marginal plants (MP) and moisture loving plants (MLP) that are ideally suited to those garden micro-climates that are temporarily or permanently wet. Within the pond environment itself, there are deep aquatics (DA) such as *Nymphaea*, floating aquatics (FA) and oxygenating plants (OP), assuming that your pond is not full of expensive to run electronics, filtering and pumping water 24/7. Many of these plants provide important sites for feeding, breeding, sheltering and hibernating for our vast range of aquatic creatures, from tiny *Daphnea* (Water fleas) to larger amphibians like frogs, newts and toads. A word of warning is needed here for those tempted by aquatic plants sold in less reputable garden centres and nurseries – there are a number of very invasive, non-native aquatic plants on sale that, if they are allowed to escape the confines of your pond, may become serious weeds in ditches, dykes and rivers. In fact some have already done so, listed below are the most invasive non-native aquatic weeds:-

Amongst many other plants that like their feet in moist or wet soil, Rodgersia pinnata 'Superba', with its purplish bronze young foliage, is a wonderful plant for boggy situations.

Crassula helmsii (Australian Swamp Stonecrop), *Fallopia japonica* (Japanese Knotweed), *Heracleum mantagazzianum* (Giant Hogweed), *Hydrocotyle ranunculoides* (Floating pennywort), *Impatiens glandulifera* (Himalayan Balsam), *Ludwigia* spps (Creeping water primrose), *Myriophyllum aquaticum* (Parrot's feather).

The government's Environment Agency has produced a very good leaflet to guide the public and contractors on how to manage these weeds and the Royal Horticultural Society has an excellent advisory page on its website. Plants worthy of consideration for an aquatic environment include:

Acorus calamus (MP), *Aponogeton distachys* (FA), *Aruncus dioicus* (MLP), *Ceratophyllum demersum* (OP), *Cimicifuga simplex* (MLP), *Filipendula* spps (MLP), *Hosta* spps (MLP), *Iris* spps (MLP / MP), *Lagarosiphon major*, (OP), *Astilbe* spps (MLP), *Lysichiton americanus* (MP), *Menyanthes trifoliata* (MP), *Mimulus* spps (MLP), *Nymphaea* spps (DA), *Nymphoides peltata* (FA), *Persicaria bistorta* (MLP), *Polygonum amphibium* (FA), *Pontaderia cordata* (MP), *Potamogeton crispus* (OP), *Primula* spps (MLP), *Ranunculus lingua* (MP), *Rodgesia* spps (MLP), *Sagittaria latifolia* (MP), *Trollius* spps (MLP).

Care should be taken when selecting any of these or other aquatic plants to ensure that they are not too invasive for the size of pond and that the depth of water is suitable to the plant's needs. Normal, free-standing garden ponds should be at least 1.2 metres deep. Propagation of this group of plants is comparatively easy, given that they are all herbaceous and grow from crowns, rhizomes or stolons – division is the simplest method, done in March and April before the plants start their summer flush.

Bedding plants – these remnants of the Victorian gardening era, still seen in abundance in some parks and gardens across Britain, have evolved over the last 20 years to provide us with a much wider range, more suited to our modern style of gardening. Some new, excellent, semi-pendulous types, suited to baskets, hay ricks and containers have given us more choice and, with many being perennial, has allowed us to propagate some of our own stock. Unfortunately, many modern bedding plants have double or semi-double flowers to make them appear more extravagant and this can stop these from having any wildlife value, as bees and hoverflies make unsuccessful attempts

These Begonia trials being carried out at RHS Gardens Wisley show us that summer bedding plants, in all their strange and spectacular guises are still as popular now as they were in Victorian times!

to access any pollen and nectar that may be present in the flowers. Choose the single flowered or multiple floretted ones to help support our insect populations. Few people still grow their own bedding plants from seed these days, given that the seed companies now supply seedlings and plantlets, sometimes known as plug plants, through the post but many of the container and basket plants can be propagated easily by cuttings taken from overwintered specimens in February and March in a heated glasshouse.

Biennials – one of the often-forgotten groups of plants in our gardens that contains some worthy plants for wildlife gardens, let alone the ornamental ones. By definition they usually flower in the early part of summer from April to late June, giving their seeds a chance to germinate and grow, before autumn, to a size capable of surviving the winter. The rather haphazard self-seeding habit of some may be one of the reasons why people do not use them as much as they could but, once you have learnt to 'control' this aspect of their two year life cycle, you can have a lot of fun with them and the associated wildlife will thank you for your efforts. Some may require a little help to get them to germinate in a cold frame or cold glasshouse but all are worthy of that extra help and will reward your efforts. Examples to look out for include:-

> *Althaea rosea* (Hollyhock), *Anthriscus sylvestris* (Cow parsley), *Aquilegia* hybrids (Columbine), *Astragalus glycyphyllos* (Milk Vetch), *Caruus nutans* (Musk Thistle), *Cheiranthus cheiri* (Wallflower), *Cynoglossum amabile* (Hounds Tongue), *Daucus carota* (Wild Carrot), *Dianthus barbatus* (Sweet William), *Digitalis purpurea* (Foxglove), *Dipsacus fullonum* (Teasle), *Echium russicum* (Viper's Bugloss), *Fibigia clypeata, Glaucium flavum* (Horned Poppy), *Hesperis matronalis* (Sweet Rocket), *Lunaria annua* (Honesty), *Meconopsis regia, Melandrium rubrum* (Red Campion), *Myosotis* spp. (Forget-me-not), *Nonea lutea, Oenothera biennis* (Evening Primrose), *Onopordum acanthium* (Cotton Thistles), *Papaver nudicaule, Peucedanum verticillare, Reseda luteola* (Dyer's Rocket), *Salvia sclarea* (Clary), *Seseli libanotis* (Moon Carrot), *Smyrnium perfoliatum* (Alexanders), *Verbascum* spp. (Mullein).

Keep in mind that all Brassicas are biennials and, if left overwinter to grow into their second year, will produce thousands of yellow Brassica flowers for bees, hoverflies and other beneficial insects to enjoy. You can then remove them once the flowers have finished as you would with any other true biennial. Leave unused Leeks to do the same thing.

One of true biennials, Digitalis purpurea (foxglove) is synonymous with early summer and the bumble bees that seem to enjoy climbing up the flower tubes to get their nectar and pollen fix. Given a relaxed approach to gardening, they will self-seed after the bees have done their work.

Tulipa (Tulip) hybrids must be one of the most spectacular spring bulbs we have but many do not naturalise themselves very well.

However, Cyclamen coum, like its autumn flowering cousin, seeds itself well, given the right conditions and is left undisturbed.

Bulbs and other storage organs – within this generic title I have included all underground storage organs – bulbs, corms, rhizomes and tubers. Before you ask, we do need to know the difference between them because that knowledge helps us to care for them and propagate from them. One of the delights of these underground storage organs is that, even for the better gardeners, their presence is often forgotten until they pop their heads above the soil to give their annual performance, in whichever season their DNA says they should. Because of the tremendous range of them available to us these days, we can enjoy these surprises at almost any time of the year, from autumn or spring *Cyclamen* to winter *Aconitums*, spring *Galanthus* and summer *Alliums* and, in doing so, any passing insects may be able to take advantage of the pollen and nectar source across the seasons. Although you may have to buy bulbs in, if you want new species or cultivars, once you have established a good 'clump' of them, you can lift them in their dormant season and replant the babies elsewhere in the garden or you can share some with your neighbours. The list below includes spring (Sp), summer (Su), Autumn (A) and Winter (W) flowering species and covers the range of storage organs – bulbs (B), corms (C), rhizomes (R) and tubers (T). By the time you have added a few of these to your garden, it will spring a surprise for you in every season and will help to support more wildlife that can appear at almost every time of year. *Allium* spps (Sp, Su, B), *Anemone blanda* and *A. nemorosa* (Sp, T), *Arum italicum* (Sp, T), *Camassia* spps (Sp, B), *Chionodoxa* spps (Sp, B), *Colchicum autumnale* (Au, B), *Convallaria majalis* (Sp, R), *Crocus* spps (Sp, C), *Cyclamem* spps (Sp, A, W, C), *Eranthis hyemalis* and *E. nivalis* (W, Sp, T), *Erythronium* spps (Sp, B), *Frittillaria* spps (Sp, Su, B), *Galanthus* (Sp, B), *Gladiolus* spps (Su, C), *Hermodactylus tuberosa* (Sp, T), *Hyacinthoides non-scripta* (Sp, B), *Hyacinthus* spps (Sp, B), *Ipheion uniflorum* (Sp, B), *Iris* spps (Sp, Su, B, R), *Ixia* spps (Sp, Su, C), *Leucojum* spps (Sp, B), *Lilium* spps (Su, B), *Muscari* spps (Sp, B0, *Narcissus* (Sp, B), *Nerine* spps (Su, A, B), *Ornithogalum* spps (Sp, Su, B), *Oxalis* spps (Sp, Su, B, R, T), *Puschkinia scilloides* (Sp, B), *Scilla* spps (Sp, B), *Sternbergia lutea* (A, B), *Trillium* spps (Sp, R), *Triteleia* spps (Sp, Su, C), *Tulipa* (Sp, B). Within each of these examples there are many species and hybrids to select from.

Climbers – whether they are woody, perennial monsters like *Rosa* 'Kiftsgate' or better behaved annual ones such as *Lathyrus odoratus,* we seem to need these rambling and scrambling plants in our gardens. For many people, climbers seem to be an excuse to erect some strange piece of iron or woodwork in their garden, only for them then to spend their time cutting the climbers back because they are preventing access to another part of the garden. Climbers naturally do what the title suggests – climb. This implies that in a totally wild environment, they will climb up another plant or scramble over a rock or cliff face. We should remember this when we are choosing climbers and when we are selecting a suitable place in our gardens. A well established tree or large shrub can make a wonderful climbing frame for the right climber, enhancing the effects of both plants. Examples of worthy climbers to look out for include: *Actinidia* spps. (Kiwi fruit), *Adlumia fungosa* (Mountain Fringe), Akebia quinata, *Asparagus verticillatus*, *Campsis radicans* (Trumpet Vine), *Celastrus orbiculatus*, *Clematis* spps, *Cobaea scandens* (Cup and Saucer Vine) *Dicentra macrocapnos*, *Eccremocarpos scaber* (Chilean Glory Flower), *Humulus lupulus* (Hop), *Ipomoea* spps (Morning Glory), *Lapageria rosea* (Chilean Bellflower), *Lathyrus odoratus* (Sweet Pea), *Lonicera* spps (Honeysuckle), *Passiflora* spps (Passion Flower), *Rhodichiton atropurpureum* (Purple Bell Vine), *Rosa* spps (Climbing and rambling roses), *Thunbergia alata* (Black-eyed Susan), *Tropaeolum* spps (Nasturtium) and *Wisteria* spps. Some of these listed above may require winter protection and some are only grown as annuals but all will provide you with a wonderful display of flowers that will support your local wildlife as well. The annuals of course can all be grown from seed but the perennials will either have to be purchased or you might try some propagation from home harvested seed, cuttings or even layering.

Wisteria sinensis is one of the most popular early summer flowering climbing, with its pendant racemes of lightly scented lilac flowers. Loved by bees, the flowers may be followed by pods reminiscent of peas or beans.

Fruit – these days, fruit, in all its strange guises, is much easier to manage and, with such a wide choice, there is no excuse. Because of the variable climate of the UK, from the sunny South East to the rainy and cool North West, it is beholden on all of us to source our fruit plants, canes, bushes and trees from 'local' suppliers that not only know our local climate but are also able to supply us with cultivars that suit the soil and climate. Here in the North of England, we have a superb organisation called the Northern Fruit Group and nationally, The Brogdale Trust, based in Kent, is a worthy organisation to use in your searches for suppliers, varieties and

A wonderful plate of Ribes uva-crispa 'Just Betty' (Gooseberry) ready for the judges, or even better, the pot! This variety has been renowned for its suitability to the show bench and the scales.

information. Propagation of many fruit types is best left to the professionals apart from Fragaria (Strawberries), Ribes (Currants) and Rubus (Raspberries) which for most gardeners should present little difficulty.

Fungi – although not a plant in the recognisable sense, fungi are not always the thugs that we imagine, leaving black marks on the leaves of our roses or destroying tiny seedlings that we have nurtured. There are many hundreds, if not thousands, of fungi that provide us and our gardens with untold and often unseen benefits. The two groups that are of benefit to us and our gardens are the saprophytic fungi that breakdown dead vegetative material in our gardens and compost heaps, releasing goodness as they do so, and the mycorrhizal fungal organisms that attach themselves to the roots of plants and help them to extract water and food, whilst benefitting from the support of the plant. So, the next time that you see a tiny toadstool in your lawn or some strange fungal organisms erupting out of a border, don't despair and reach for the nearest fungicide; see if you can identify it and check whether it is actually a beneficial fungus. Of course, you can also pop down to your local greengrocers and buy 500 grams of chestnut mushrooms for your dinner as well! Read more on this fascinating but sometimes confusing subject in Chapter Nine on pests, diseases etc.

Grasses – this group of plants has increased in their importance as garden and landscape plants throughout the 1990s and 2000s, as they require a minimum of maintenance, will cope with many different soil conditions and

This bracket fungus, unidentified, is attacking an old tree stump. Some are parasitic, killing the host plant and some are saprophytic, rotting down the remaining plant material, recycling it into the soil as organic matter.

Amanita muscaria, the Fly Agaric, is one of many fungi that live symbiotically with other plants, in this case Betula (Birch) and Pinus (Pine) species. WARNING! This fungi that appears usually in the autumn in dangerously poisonous.

are not prone to pest or disease attack like many other groups of plants. The Family, Poaceae, contains the cereal crops that sustain most of the planets population and, in our own small pieces of Planet Earth, provide all-year-round colour and interest as well as supporting many birds species with its seeds and nesting material. Of course, it also provides us with our lawns and a number of nuisance weeds. Bamboo, as one of the large members of the family, also provides building material in some parts of the world. See Appendix 1 for a list of good and bad examples.

Hardy Annuals – my favourite group of plants for the natural garden and the organic gardener. Easy to sow, easy to grow and easy to get rid of – what more can we ask for? With no need for fertilizers or watering, and no requirements for complex soil

Cortederia selloana (Pampas Grass) is perhaps one of the larger and most well known grass species seen in our gardens.

Helianthus annus (Sunflower), is perhaps the most widely known of all hardy annuals, producing flowers for us and the bees to enjoy and then producing seeds and cooking oils for us and the birds to enjoy. Everyone is a winner.

preparations, what more could you want. As most of our hardy annuals produce simple, single flowers over several months, they are ideal for supporting a wide variety of insects. In addition, some will produce dry flowers and seed heads for dried flower arrangements, let alone cut flowers. See Appendix 1 for more details on species to look out for. Some of these may become biennial in their habit, germinating before the end of summer and flowering in late spring and so further extending the flowering season of this delightful group of plants.

Hedging – this subject has been addressed elsewhere in the book but, suffice it to say that, with hindsight, I suspect that many of us have learnt our lesson over the use of vigorous, ugly, single species coniferous hedges so popular in the latter half of the last century. At least, I hope so!

Herbaceous perennials – of all the plant groups that we might choose from, these are probably the most popular in our modern gardens. Spanning the seasons from the earliest *Helleborus* (Hellebores) in January to the late flowering *Asters* (Michaelmas Daisies) in November, there are examples to suit every pocket, every gardener, every garden, ever soil and every environment. Our attitude to the care of these garden delights has evolved over recent years, with the ideas of Piet Oudolf and Professor Nigel Dunnett and his colleague Professor James Hitchmough from The University of Sheffield affecting our plant choice, planting styles and management techniques. Cutting down in autumn is now considered to be not necessary for many species as both the gardener and the wildlife that chose to visit the garden benefit from the stems and seed-heads throughout the dormant season, whenever that may be. The range of species covers so many different aspects of our gardens and so, to help you decipher the maze of information, I have coded each plant:-

D = prefers dry soils,

Div = easy to propagate by division of crown,

H = hardy,

M = prefers moist soils,

R = rampant

S = sun loving

Se = easy to propagate by seed

Sh = shade loving

T = tender

W = excellent for supporting pollinating insects

Acanthus spps (Bears breeches) (Div, H)

Achillea spps (Yarrow) (D, Div, H, S, Se, W)

Aconitum (Monkshood) (D, H, Sh, W, Poisonous)

Actaea spps (Bugbane) (Div, H, M, Sh, W)

Agapanthus spps (African Blue Lily) (Div, H, S, Se, W)

Alchemilla spp (Lady's Mantle) (Div, H, M, Se, We)

Allium spps (Onion) (H, S, Se, We)

Anchusa spps (Alkanet) (D, H, S, Se, W)

Anemone spps (Windflower) (varies across the species)

Anthemis spps (D, Div, H, S, Se, W)

Asphodelus spps(Asphodel) (D, Div, H, S, Se, W)

Aster spps (varies across the species)

Astilbe spps (Ac, Div, H, M, Sh, W)

Astrantia spps (Hatty's Pincushion) (Div, H, M, S, Se, Sh, W)

Bergenia spps (Elephant's Ears) (D, Div, H, S, Se, Sh, W)

Brunnera spps (Div, H, M, Se, Sh, W), *Campanula* spps (Bellflower) (varies across the species)

Centaurea spps (Knapweeds) (D, Div, H, S, Se, W)

Cephalaria gigantea (Giant Scabious) (D, D, H, S, Se, W)

Coreopsis spps (Tickseed) (D, Div, H, S, Se, W)

Crocosmia spps (Montbretia) (D, Div, H, R, S, Se, W)

Doronicum spps (Leopard's Bane) (Div, H, M, S, Se, W)

Echinacea spps (Coneflower) (D, Div, H, S, Se, W)

Echinops (D, Div, H, S, Se, W),

Epimedium spps (Bishop's Mitre) (D, Div, H, Se, Sh, W)

Erigeron spps (Fleabane) (D, Div, H, S, Se, W)

Eryngium spps (Sea Holly) (D, Div, H, S, Se, W)

Euphorbia spps (Spurge) (varies across the species)

Geranium spps (Cranesbill) (varies across the species)

Geum spps (Avens) (D, Div, M, S, Se, W)

Helenium spps (Helen's Flower) (D, Div, H, S,Se, W)

Helianthus spps (Sunflower) (D, Div, H, S, Se, W)

Helleborus spps (Hellebore) (Div, H, M, Se, Sh, W)

Heuchera spps (Coral Flower) (varies across the species)

Inula spps (varies across the species), *Iris* spps (varies across the species)

Knautia spps (Field Scabious) (D, H, S, Se, W)

Kniphofia (Red Hot Poker) (D, Div, H, S, Se, W)

Lamium spps (Dead Nettles) (D, Div, H, R, Se, Sh, W)

Ligularia spps (Div, H, M, S, Se, Sh, W)

Lychnis spps (Campion) (D, Div, H, S, Se, Sh, W)

Lysimachia spps (Loosestrife) (varies across the species)

Monarda spps (Bergamot) (Div, H, M, S, Se, Sh, W)

Omphalodes spps (Navelwort) (Div, H, M, Sh, W)

Origanum spps (Oregano) (D, Div, H, S, Se, W)

Penstemon spps (D, H, S, Se, W)

Persicaria spps (varies across the species)

Phlox spps (varies across the species)

Physostegia spps (Obedient plant) (Div, H, M, S, Se, W)

Polemonium (Jacob's Ladder) (Div, H, M, S, Se, W)

Potentilla spps (Cinquefoil) (D, Div, H, S, Se, W)

Primula spps (Primrose) (varies across the species)

Pulmonaria spps (Lungwort) (Div, H, M, Se, Sh, W)

Ranunculus spps (Buttercup) (varies across the species)

Salvia spps (Sage) (D, H, S, Se, W)

Scabious spps (Pincushion flower) (D, Div, H, S, Se, W)

Sedum spps (Stonecrop) (D, D, H, S, Se, W)

Symphytum spps (Comfrey) (Div, H, M, R, S, Se, Sh, W)

Tanacetum spps (Tansy / Pyrethrum) (D, Div, H, S, Se, W)

Thalictrum spps (Meadow Rue) (Div, H, M, S, Se, W)

Trollius spps (Globeflower) (Div, H, M, S, Se, W)

Verbascum spps (Mullein) (D, Div, H, S, Se, W)

Veronica spps (Speedwell) (varies across the species)

Viola spps (Violet) (varies across the species)

To follow the list further for plants that will attract and support wildlife in a variety of ways, the RHS has a downloadable, comprehensive list on its website called 'Plants for Pollinators' that is worth carrying with you when you visit Gardens, Garden Centres and Nurseries.

Herbs – because of the upsurge in culinarily related television programmes and books over recent years, the sale of herbs has taken off, as plants and seeds from garden centres, dried herbs in supermarkets, pot grown fresh herbs in supermarkets and herbal preparations from health food shops. I do wonder how many of these modern variations on the word herb, when compared with

The spectacular herbaceous perennial *Helleborus x hybridus (Lenten Lily)* is continuing to throw up wonderful new colours, giving our gardens a spectacular display in later winter and early spring. The flowers support early flying bumble bees and then set seed.

Cephalaria gigantea, the Giant Scabious is amongst the best herbaceous perennials for supporting bees in early summer.

Lavendula angustifolia (Common Lavender) is excellent for supporting bees and butterflies searching out nectar and pollen. We can use the results of their hard work in the form of seeds in Lavender oils, Lavender bags and even in Lavender cake.

our 15th to 19th century forebears, are actually used! Most of us will only ever use around six different herbs for culinary purposes and very few will find an aromatic or medicinal use for them, mainly because we have lost a lot of the knowledge that previous generations took for granted. One of the best reference books of recent years on this subject is the RHS Encyclopaedia of Herbs and, for those that wish to take the subject further, I suggest that you treat yourself to it. Suffice it to say that many of our commonly grown herbs, giving a very sunny position and a well-drained soil, will not only satisfy your needs but will also provide support for a wide variety of wildlife. Just watch honey bees and other wild bees working in a field of *Lavendula* (Lavender). For an excellent day trip from most parts of Yorkshire, visit Yorkshire Lavender near Terrington in North Yorkshire during the summer months. See Appendix 6 for details.

Roses – of all the changes in the gardening world in the last 30 years, roses have surely gone through the most. One of the alarm bells rang when the Royal National Rose Society announced that it was selling off a major part of their gardens near St. Albans in Hertfordshire and using the newly acquired funds to totally revamp the remaining gardens. The RNRS has since ceased to operate. Gone are the days of beds full of single varieties of Hybrid Tea or Floribunda roses, as they use to be called. David Austin has done more to revitalise the development, sale and use of roses than almost any other British rose breeder and we can now see roses as an integral part of our mixed gardens rather than an isolated feature that flowers for around 2 weeks in July and 2 weeks in September, leaving the remaining 48 weeks of the year completely blank. We now have much longer flowering periods, repeat flowering, scent, disease resistance, less routine pruning and spraying and much happier gardeners. As with herbs above, I would recommend that you treat yourself to the RHS Encyclopaedia of Roses to get the true picture of roses across the centuries and into the modern day.

Shrubs – from tiny *Hebes* to monstrous *Mahonias*, the world of shrubs is perhaps larger than any other group of plants apart from herbaceous perennials. The variations include deciduous, evergreen, spreading, upright, ball shaped, suitable for clipping and requiring no clipping at all. One of the big mistakes that we all make when selecting a new shrub for our gardens is not reading the label to find out what the ultimate height and spread will be. The result is that these unsuspecting plants, after five or six years of giving us their performance, are hit with the hedge trimmer to 'control' them and we never see the true beauty of the shrub ever again. With the right choice of plant and the correct method of pruning, many of our shrubs will give upwards of 20 years valuable service. Remember also that many shrubs can support a wide diversity of wildlife, from honey bees searching for pollen and nectar to a visiting butterfly looking for a quick nectar fix. Birds use shrubs for shelter, protection, nesting and feeding. If you are limited for space, why not grown one or two shrubs as wall shrubs – *Ribes rubrum* (Red and White Currants) cultivars do particularly well on shaded walls and fences. If you read through Appendix 1, you will find more ideas on shrubs that can support wildlife whilst also giving you and your neighbour's pleasure.

Trees – I am often asked to give people ideas on trees for small gardens and I duly respond with six or seven examples, commonly available through reputable outlets. Conversely, I also hear comments about what a nuisance trees are – they drop leaves, berries, bird droppings and honeydew from vast populations of aphid in early summer. They upset drives and paths, let alone blocking light from windows – these excuses are because most trees are planted in the wrong places and the choice of species is wrong. If every garden in Britain were to plant one tree, of a suitable species, in a suitable position, we could have several million more trees to support a huge diversity of wildlife, feed us and soak up some of that destructive CO_2. Go on, plant a tree. The Tree Council organises a huge number of events each year as part of National Tree Week, normally at the end of November and early December and has been doing so since 1975. Here are some examples of trees that most small to medium gardens can manage, given the right attitude of mind of the owner:- *Acer campestre, A.griseum* and *A.negundo, Amelanchier* spps, *Betula utilis, Crataegus* spps, *Malus* spps, *Sorbus aucuparia.* It is best to avoid *Prunus* (flowering cherries) although there are species such as P. *incisa, sargentii, serrula* and s*ubhirtella* that are less invasive than the rather gaudy, larger Japanese Flowering Cherries. Search out trees with a fastigiate habit of growth that do not take up much width in the garden and, if all else fails, choose trees that are productive and / or that can be trained onto a fence or wall, remembering that some are grafted onto dwarfing rootstocks to help restrict their ultimate size.

Vegetables – if this latest bug has not bitten you yet, it soon will, as we are progressively encouraged to grow at least some of our own vegetables for ourselves and our families and then eat five of them every day. With the hundreds of thousands of hectares currently occupied by domestic gardens, the nation's, if not the world's, food shortage could be resolved just by each of us with a garden growing a few vegetables and salad crops. This helps to ensure that the healthy eating advice is followed better; we all get a little more fresh air and exercise and

This true rambling rose, Rosa 'Turner's Crimson Rambler', is a good mid-summer rose suited to the smaller garden.

Ribes speciosa, the Fuchsia-flowered currant, is a wonderful example of a mid-spring flowering currant that is good as a wall shrub or a free-standing shrub, much loved by bumble bees. Their hard work results in bright red fruits.

Amelanchier lamarckii, the Snowy Mespilus, seen here at Thorp Perrow Arboretum near Bedale, with its racemes of pure white flowers that can be followed by purple-black fruits as well as stunning orange and red autumn colour, can be grown as a multi-stemmed larger shrub or small tree.

A commercial crop of tomatoes in a glasshouse in East Yorkshire, managed without the use of inorganic pesticides – the flowers are pollinated by bumblebees from imported hives. Not organic but very close to it.

we can feel that we are adding something to the other side of the apparent world food shortage equation. When selecting vegetables and salad crops to grow in your garden, discuss what you want to grow with your family and also your neighbours so that gluts of seedlings and crops can be shared across the garden fence. Look out for cultivars that help you to reduce your use of pesticides by their natural resistance or immunity to diseases and pests. Many seed catalogues now give excellent details about varieties that have a proven level of resistance to one disease or another.

Chapter Seven

The Answer
Lies in the Soil

Minerals in the soil control the metabolism of plants, animals and man. All of life is either healthy or unhealthy according to the fertility of the soil.

Nobel Prize Winner Dr. Alexus Carrel. (1912)

WHAT MORE NEEDS to be said? This quote from 100 + years ago has as much relevance in today's world as it did in those heady days before the First World War, as we see the world rushing headlong into an irreversible human and climatic disaster of Biblical proportions. The Great American Dust-bowl of the late 1930s should have taught us all a lesson about soil conservation and management but sadly, and with typical human arrogance, we ignored it and many other apparently lesser examples before and since. Check out the details of why the Mesopotamian civilisation disappeared and why, in the early part of the 21st Century, the San Joaquin Valley in California is struggling to grow crops anymore!

Soil is the basis of all life along with water – lose them and we cannot feed ourselves; neglect them and the food we eat will have little real nutritional value. Whichever way you look at it, if we do not conserve and care for this strange brown metamorphic mixture, all human life on the planet will cease to exist. 2015 was the United Nations International Year of Soils and was intended to help the world see soils as the most important material on the planet. Suggestions by some scientists that the world has less than 50 more harvests before we destroy this complex material seem to have fallen on deaf ears. The Climate Conference in Paris in December 2015 hardly gave mention to it!

All those who manage plants, whether they be agriculturists, horticulturists, environmentalists, foresters, greenkeepers, ecologists or gardeners, must learn to respect the importance of soil and then learn how to care for it and all the trillions of living organisms that live in it.

Words like "mud" and "dirt" are used by those that do not understand this strange and complex brown mixture. It has an infinitely variable recipe, with thousands of ingredients in various proportions, held together in hundreds of different ways and is sometimes likened to recipes for cakes – get the mixture of ingredients right and you have a cake that everyone wants a piece of; get the ingredients wrong and even the birds that visit your garden will not eat it. Get the recipe for the soil right and it will grow the best plants; get the recipe wrong and you will never succeed.

The basic ingredients are:- Mineral content – sand, silt and clay particles in various ratios, humus and its derivative organic matter in various stages of decomposition, water and dissolved nutrients, air and a whole host of living organisms in all their rich diversity.

One of the current problems for all gardeners and growers with the new generation of multi-purpose composts, made from the infinitely variable municipal green waste, with its chemical residues from our gardens, and other non-peat based organic materials, is that the basic ingredients are not behaving in the same way as ordinary, healthy garden soil or even peat-based composts. They are not a substitute for soil or peat-based composts and, at the present rate of 'improvement', never will be. Compost producers have tried out the coconut waste, Coir, that has had to travel halfway across the planet to reach us, composted straw that may be polluted with fungicide, herbicide and insecticide residues and pulverised bark from the forestry industry – like soils, their value as compost materials is totally dependent upon the recipe that is used and, from reports see in recent years, they are still trying to work it out!

When it comes to managing our garden soils or multi-purpose composts, we have to remember the two basic rules of soils. Soil structure is the way in which the various ingredients are held together, and soil texture is the ratio of each ingredient to the other. So, for example, a clay soil may be expected to have upwards of 50% clay particles in it and therefore we might expect it to have a heavy structure, with poor drainage but good nutrient retention.

Despite what you may have been told, it is difficult, expensive and wasteful to try to change the raw mineral ingredients in a garden or the natural soil texture, although in containers and raised beds it is easy. So, with a clay soil, although adding coarse sand or even gravel may seem to improve drainage, you are unlikely to be able to change the sub-soil or bed rock from which the top soil has been formed and so it will only be shallow rooted plants that will benefit and only then until the autumn rains bring the water table to the surface. A relatively modern saying "don't fight it, enjoy it" sums up the attitude that an organic gardener will take to the soil.

CLAY SOILS

Some years ago, when we lived in Nottingham, I watched a neighbour, with a gently sloping garden, dig out all the heavy, grey Nottinghamshire clay from his back garden and replace it with imported 'top soil.' When, a few months later, we had a period of very heavy rain, for what seemed like weeks, his garden filled up with the surface water running in from surrounding gardens and it became an unmanageable bog for months. I battled with the same clay soil for five years and eventually I won – lots of hard work, tonnes of organic matter and a very healthy garden(er) – I remember that raspberries, roses, brassicas and sweet peas did particularly well in this clay soil.

Although clay soils are the most difficult to manage because they dry out, shrink and crack in summer and become wet and gluey in winter, they are, once the battle has been won, the richest of all soils. Nutrients levels are high because little leaching can take place, water levels are generally high because of poor drainage and, for stronger rooted plants, they are held firm in the soil and so perform better.

On the flip side of that equation, they can dry out to a material resembling a brick in a dry summer and the vertical cracks that appear at the surface can tear tree roots apart deeper down in the sub-soil. Having had to manage two gardens in Nottinghamshire with very heavy clay soils, I have learnt one or two serious lessons in my working and domestic lives and know that, in the end, there is no substitute for the addition of copious amounts of well-rotted organic matter and correct timing of any deeper cultivation works, usually together – namely in early autumn, before the soil gets too heavy and before any autumn and winter frosts. The soil structure can then be broken open by the effects of frosts and rain.

SILTY SOILS

These alluvial soils, left as deposits from old and young river estuaries, are amongst the best soils for cultivation and moisture retention but are amongst the worst for erosion. Drive through parts of East and North Yorkshire after heavy rain or during springtime agricultural soil cultivations and watch the amount of soil that is washed or blown away. In our gardens these soils cap over very quickly after any surface cultivation, leaving the soil with poor air circulation and sometimes stopping seeds from germinating. These symptoms occur because the individual particles of soil are rounded in shape, allowing them to 'roll' easily and thus making them unstable. The texture of silty soils is usually silky and the structure is often weak, with the soil not forming large crumbs unless there is plenty of humus to stick the particles together.

Management of these soils in our gardens is best done by dense planting to stop the soil from being battered by the weather, mulching of open soils overwinter to help prevent erosion and leaving any deeper cultivations for vegetables until spring, by which time any mulches will have worked their way into the soil with the aid of the weather and worms. Green manures are one type of winter mulch that works well with silty soils, sown in autumn and dug in during early spring cultivations.

Sandy soils

Having experienced the opposite end of the soil spectrum in Nottinghamshire, we moved to an area just south of Huddersfield in 1984 and discovered sandy soils that produced a totally different pedological challenge. The bed rock of this part of the Pennines is sedimentary millstone grit and sandstone and, apart from one or two strange pockets of clay, caused by geological disturbances millions of years ago, the top soil texture is, for the most part, a very coarse sandy loam, with almost no true structure. Large, fist size boulders of crumbly sandstone can be found within 30 cm of the surface, with top quality building and paving sandstone deeper into the bed rock. The soil water drains before your very eyes, taking Nitrogen and Calcium with it in large quantities – this phenomenon gives us the acidic peat moorlands of the South Pennines on our doorstep.

Cross to the area around Selby, only 30 miles away and a very different sandy soil is common – it is a fine sandy loam that can grow root crops forever and a day. Both soils are light, easily dug and will warm up quickly in spring because there is less water in the soil to heat up. Both soils will eat organic matter in vast quantities and neither soil will benefit from autumn cultivation – better to mulch with one of the many green manures or farmyard manure (FYM) to help prevent winter erosion and then to cultivate in springtime, if you choose to use the more traditional methods of soil management. A no-dig philosophy might be a better way to manage sandy soils, only turning the soil over as part of any planting or sowing practices.

NUTRIENTS, SOIL WATER, pH, PORE SPACES, ORGANIC MATTER AND SOIL ORGANISMS

These six essential elements of soils and composts are studied in great depth by pedologists, agriculturists, horticulturists and greenkeepers because they form the basis of successful 'crops.' For amateur gardeners, the science of soils (pedology) is a complex mystery that is probably best left alone unless you are particularly interested. Unfortunately, it cannot be ignored and we can waste water, food and plants by getting these elements of soil management wrong.

Nutrients – of all the ingredients in soils, this must be the most complex. Look at the periodic table and count the number of elements – the current table, at the time of writing this piece, suggests 118 different elements that have been isolated, identified and named from Hydrogen (1) to Oganesson (118). Imagine all of those, in various quantities being provided in a bag of fertilizer. Impossible in any ordinary soil, in the soil water, as part of the organic matter (humus) or as an ingredient in a soil particle. But, a vast array of them are essential to all forms of plant life, whether growing in the wild or in our cultivated gardens. The big three, the macro-nutrients, Nitrogen (N), Phosphorous (P) and Potassium (K) are the major elements for good plant growth, including foliage growth, flowering, seed germination and fruit / seed development, hardiness, disease resistance etc. These form the basis of all general fertilisers used in our garden as dry or liquid preparations, whether they are organic or inorganic in their origins. The secondary elements include Magnesium (Mg), that is essential for the continued production of Chlorophyll in leaves, and Calcium (Ca) that is essential for the movement of water in plants. The micro-elements include Iron (Fe), Manganese (Mn), Copper (Cu) and Zinc (Zn).

Organic matter – now here is a subject that could fill a whole chapter all on its own. As every living organism is born, grows, urinates, defecates and dies, it sheds a disproportionate amount of waste material that is either directly consumed by another organism or is attacked by the various agents of decomposition – rain, fungi, bacteria etc. The resulting materials become an integral part of the soil, the rivers and the seas. This of course includes all flora as well as all fauna – the biota of our planet. In the natural world this process goes on unseen and largely ignored by most humans.

In our intensive 'crop' production we have chosen to use some of the more easily accessible waste to help improve the organic matter content of our soils – farmyard manure in its various forms, leaf mould, garden compost, peat, coir, forest bark, soot, bonfire ash and even our own human waste! All of these materials add nutrients, soil organisms and humus – the end product of decomposed organic matter that is said to be black and sticky – it adheres to soil particles, helping to form a better soil structure and thus reducing the possibilities of soil erosion as well as water and nutrient loss by leaching. All those benefits from a relatively small amount of organic matter. Wow! For anyone considering going down the organic route in their own gardens, take care when sourcing bulky organic matter from 'the farm gate.' Has the farmer used herbicides on the pastures that the animals feed on? Has the farmer used pesticides on the crops that the animals feed on? Has the farmer used antibiotics on the animals that create the bulky manures?

Composting – everyone has their own recipe and technique for getting that wonderful brown gold out of biodegradable green garden and kitchen waste and I do not intend to teach my grandmother to suck eggs by instructing the reader in the ultimate way to get the best, fastest and most useable garden compost. However, there are one or two golden rules that will help the novice and less experienced gardeners to get the best results with the least inconvenience – after all, there is nothing worse than opening up a compost heap after that 6 month wait, only to find a stinking, anaerobic mess inside.

In the UK, our climate is classified as cool temperate and as such cannot be relied on to provide the necessary constant high temperature for the bacteria that are a part of the decomposition process, particularly in our relatively small, typically 1 cubic metre garden compost heaps to do their job. On an industrial scale, where the green waste that we take to the tip is processed in heaps that may contain 1000s of cubic metres, bacteria can build up into unbelievable numbers, generating their own heat and becoming the dominant agent for decomposition, alongside fungal agents – the heat can build up to such a point that spontaneous combustion can occur – this will not happen in your average garden compost heap. Worms do not form an important part of this essential industrial scale process but in our own gardens, where large scale composting is neither feasible, desirable or necessary, unless it is part of a community composting activity, the humble brandling worm, *Eisenia fetida*, is one of the most important agents, acting at much lower temperatures than bacteria but requiring a rather specialised environment that we forget at our peril.

We must construct compost heaps that have an aerobic environment, a pH above 7 and a mix of ingredients that includes carboniferous and nitrogenous material so that the brandling worms can feed and breed in sufficient numbers to process the materials quickly, whilst you continue to add a fresh supply to the top. Take care not to add too much of any one material at a time as this may create a chemical imbalance – avoid acidic grass clippings unless they are thoroughly mixed with drier, carboniferous material such as shredded paper and do not add dense hedge clippings in one go as these can settle and become anaerobic. Do not intentionally include any material that is infected with fungal, bacterial or viral diseases as these are unlikely to be killed out in the garden compost heap because it does not, necessarily, get hot enough – an old guide line was 180°C to kill out unwanted pathogens in soils being sterilised for potting composts – very unlikely in the average garden compost heap, even in the height of summer.

Other agents that will do some of the work for you include bacteria, fungi, woodlice and several species of slugs, these in turn attracting predatory ground beetles, centipedes and hedgehogs, with field mice adding to the diversity as they feed on vegetative food scraps. To help support and protect these essential agents whilst they get on with their job, it is best to keep the top of the heap covered with a waterproof sheet or lid so that any heat is preserved and that the

The remarkable Brandling Worm, Eisenia fetida, consumes vast quantities of vegetative waste in our compost heaps but needs all the conditions in the heap to be right for it to thrive and do its work.

The Yellow Slug, Limax flavus, seen here on the underside of the covering that I use on top of my heap, feeds on fungi and decomposing waste. It is not a threat to any of our garden plants!

heap does not get too wet or dry in our varied climate. To assist these agents in their work, apart from giving them a constant supply of fresh vegetative material, a light dressing of Calcium hydroxide (garden lime) two or three times a year will help to maintain the neutral to alkaline environment preferred by the worms – this helps to cancel out the acidic bi-products left by bacteria in their work. To stimulate bacteria to do their job more affectively you can add a light dressing of any high Nitrogen fertilizer once or twice a year but over-loading the heap with this can make the heap more acidic, in turn discouraging the worms – a fine balance has to be achieved!

If you have the space, two or three compost heaps will allow you to fill, cover and leave a heap for up to six months whilst the others are either being used in the garden or are being filled. The dry, apparently un-decomposed top layers of any heap are a vital source of agents, in their various stages of development, for the beginning of a new heap and should be placed at the bottom of the new heap as you begin its construction.

There are a number of schools of thought about compaction of the heap as it grows but, over-compaction will develop anaerobic conditions that so many of the important agents do not like and so should be discouraged. Natural settlement is usually enough.

The final outcome of the hard work of these agents in your heap and the little bit of help from you, after 6 - 12 months, is a material that is so vital to the biological activity and diversity of your garden and its soil that the benefits cannot be highlighted too much – used as a planting compost, it is one of the best and is, to all intents and purposes, free!

pH – we all remember the Litmus paper tests that we carried out in the Science labs at school and, for us horticulturists, these simple tests help us to understand the extremes of the pH scale. Being a logarithmic scale, the extremes of acidity and alkalinity of soils can have a serious effect on plants and the availability of essential minerals. The scale runs from 0 to 14, with 7 being considered to be the neutral point. One point down or up from that neutral point and you will find a soil that is 10 times as acid or alkaline. Two points down or up and it is 100 times as acid or alkaline.

There are groups of plants that have a preference for acid or alkaline soils. Calcifuges do not like alkaline soils and calcicoles prefer alkaline soils.

Calcifuge examples include: *Calluna, Camellia, Daboecia, Erica, Gentiana, Kalmia, Meconopsis, Pieris, Rhododendron, Solanum* and *Vaccinium*.

Calcicole examples include: *Brassica, Buddleia, Buxus, Campanula,*

Ceanothus, Cistus, Clematis, Dianthus, Euonymus, Fagus, Fraxinus, Geranium, Hebe, Lavendula, Taxus and *Viburnum.*

The effect of these extremes on plants is often seen when certain mineral elements become unavailable or are washed out.

We should always remember that the vast majority of ordinary garden plants can survive, if not thrive, in a wide variety of soils and so, unless your garden soil has a definite acidic or alkaline bias you need not concern yourself too much.

Pore spaces – the porosity of a compost or soil determines whether plants will survive or not. Heavy, sticky clay soils have few pore spaces for air to circulate and water to flow through. This can create anaerobic conditions that are not conducive to healthy plant growth. Sandy soils have a disproportionately high amount of pore spaces and so drain freely, losing nutrients as this process occurs.

Soil organisms – Charles Darwin classified earth worms as nature's ploughs and, as one creature that lives in our soils in various quantities, we must do all that we can to encourage them. Their work in moving organic matter into and around our soils, unseen, is a vital part of the maintenance of soils in our northern temperate gardens. Their nuisance value in lawns, when they produce

The Large Rose Sawfly larvae, seen here on Rosa glauca foliage, overwinter in the soil and emerge to mate and start the cycle again in June and July.

The incredible natural stone sculptures at the National Trust property, Brimham Rocks, are formed from sandstone that creates an acidic soil.

casts in spring and autumn, must be offset by their value as drainage experts - underground channels created by their activities are better than any aerator or garden fork in improving drainage. One unfortunate side-effect of having a healthy population of earth worms in your lawns and gardens is that moles can be attracted to this bumper harvest, causing disturbance and disruption. Livestock farmers and equestrian managers know all too well what devastating effects moles can have in a grassy field. Black birds, rooks and starlings will also take advantage of a healthy earth worm population, giving us all a good reason to encourage them! Earth worms, along with the brandling worms that we find in our compost heaps have a preference for neutral to alkaline soils and so will be more prevalent in those circumstances.

Centipedes, wireworms, chafer grubs, leatherjackets, carrot and cabbage root flies, Scarlet Lily Beetles, sawflies, winter moths, vine weevils, slugs, ground beetles, ants - all of these, and untold thousands more beneficial and detrimental creatures live in our soils in some sort of natural balance. Unfortunately, humans upset that balance without realising it. The use of pesticides, excessive cultivation, over-use of artificial fertilisers, monoculture and many other factors disrupt the natural balance of subterranean life, leaving us all wondering what has gone wrong, but never asking the question 'what have we done wrong?'

Fungal organisms – mycorrhiza, fly agarics, honey fungus, rose black spot - the same story applies here – good and bad fungi, in such variety as to be beyond human comprehension, all play their part in the life of our soils and occasionally one or other of them causes our beloved crops an often transitory problem? We do not necessarily see that many other fungal organisms have given our crops a helping hand, without asking for too much in return – a symbiotic relationship that only one party really contributes to – a little unfair, don't you think! Organic gardeners will appreciate this relationship and do as much as possible to fulfil his / her side of the symbiotic bargain.

Bacteria – untold numbers of these microscopic organisms live in our soils without us ever knowing what they are or, for that matter, what they do! It is said that there are as many bacteria in one handful of healthy soil as there are human beings on the planet – 7 billion and counting! These organisms form an essential part of the life of our soils, fixing atmospheric nitrogen in the roots of certain plants, helping to process plant, animal and human waste and so recycling the manufactured materials of life into new life. If only we were as good at this process. If you ever forget how beneficial bacteria are in the garden, just remember that our guts are full of them, both good and bad.

Soil water – of course it is not just H^2O. It is a complex solution of dissolved minerals and water that our beloved plants take in through the root hairs to help create new growth, flowers, fruits and seeds. Our task, as organic gardeners, is to try to assist in the process of making that solution available in the right mix at the right time for the plant to maximise the desired growth.

Water and nutrient conservation have been discussed above and are the starting point in any garden, container, raised bed or hanging basket. In our strange and varied Yorkshire climate, water availability, through natural rainfall, rain butts or the garden tap seldom seem to be a problem but in July 2018, the vast majority of the UK had a prolonged period of sunshine and almost no appreciable rainfall since early May. Lawns were brown, trees were shedding leaves, fruit trees were shedding embryo fruits and other susceptible plants were wilted and died before our eyes. The question for all of us is which plants need the water and which can we leave alone?

One of the big questions for all gardeners is at what time of day do you water your containers of precious flowers, fruits and vegetables? Whether you are watering tomatoes in a glasshouse of a hanging basket that is beautifying your ornamental garden, the straight answer is always first thing in the morning. It is the time of day when the plants start to need a good supply of water, the water heats up as the day goes on and so does not encourage fungal diseases and the slugs and snails have all gone back to bed so are not attracted to the smell of the water. Water at night, as many people seem to do and you get the opposite effect – cold water that stays cold all night and encourages fungi, some of the water will have drained away by morning, the plants water use is dramatically reduced overnight and the smell of water attracts slug and snails to do their dirty work at the time of day when you are fast asleep!

If those of us with properties with downfall pipes had a few more of these, there might be a little more water left in the reservoirs for other necessities!

Chapter Eight

Gadgets, Gadgets and More Gadgets

For where the old thick laurels grow, along the thin brick wall,
You find the tool and potting-sheds which are the heart of all:
The cold frame and the hot-houses, the dung pits and the tanks,
The rollers, carts and drain-pipes, with the barrows and the planks.

Rudyard Kipling (1911)
From: The Glory of the Garden

SINCE THE TIME of the Ancient Egyptians, garden tools have been invented and re-invented and have evolved to help us manage the growing of ornamental plants and crops. At their zenith in Victorian Britain, garden tools were designed and manufactured for almost every garden task. Visit any gardening museum or read any original Victorian gardening book and you will see what I mean.

Nowadays, we seem to be a little more concerned for the optional and yet 'must have' extras of gardening that help to 'beautify' our precious plots rather than providing us with the aids to manage them. How did we ever manage before solar powered garden lighting? Did our herbaceous plants just fall over and rot before we had the modern generation of 'hoops' that are seen at every garden show in the country?

Visit any garden show anywhere in Britain from March through to October and you will be bamboozled by the array of 'essential' tools, equipment and paraphernalia that we are tempted by to help us manage our ever-decreasing sized garden plots.

I have listed below my essential tools that for more than 50 years have helped me to manage my garden(s) to my satisfaction and hopefully to the satisfaction of a few others that may have strolled around the Porter estate. As you read through the list, you may choose to consider the collection of tools and equipment that you have amassed, creating a retain pile and a reject / recycle / resell / donate to charity pile – think of all the spare room that you will have in your shed or garage!

Edging shears – I own a pair for occasional use around the garden to neaten up the boundary between the lawns and the borders.

Forks – my garden fork gets used less and less these days because of the potential destruction it can do to plant roots and to larger forms of life that may be living or hibernating in the soil. I do own a smaller border fork that occasionally gets used for planting.

Garden bags – a relatively new innovation for us gardeners that makes the collection and disposal of our garden waste a lot easier. There are lots of variations in quality on the market so buy the best that you can afford as they will last you a lot longer.

Garden knife – my general-purpose garden knife is actually a pruning knife with a downward facing tip to aid the long pull needed to make a good pruning cut, if the knife is sharpened correctly. Its uses are many and varied, from cutting string and slitting open a bag of compost to cutting up the root ball of an unsuspecting herbaceous perennial if I decide to divide it up and replant it. With a good quality blade and a comfortable wooden handle, it is one of those must-haves in the gardener's pocket.

Garden shed – purchased in 1977 when we moved into our first owner-occupied house in Bramcote, Nottingham (a three bedroom semi-detached purchased for £11,000!), this £100 worth of timber and glass has satisfied me completely as a store for tools, equipment, materials etc. It has had three new roofing felt covers over that time and has been treated inside and out every three to four years with an appropriate timber preservative (not Creosote) – no rotting timber so far. Two panes of glass have been replaced in all that time and, to all intents and purposes, it is as good as new. To provide continuity in the garden, it is painted with the same forest green timber treatment that we use for the fences and gates in various part of the garden and has a Red Currant bush trained on the North-East side to add to its value and purpose.

Hand fork and trowel – good quality, stainless steel ones have lasted me for 25 years plus, with no signs of wear and tear. Essential for bulb planting, weeding and a thousand other untold tasks, too numerous to mention.

Hand shears – essential for those pieces of topiary and cloud pruning that electrical hedge trimmers are really too clumsy for.

Hedge trimmer – although I do have a pair of hand shears in my garden shed, for the major annual task of cutting my two mixed species boundary hedges and my *Buxus* (Box) hedge, an electric one is my current tool of choice. Hedge trimming is its only task and no individual shrub has ever had the implement anywhere near it. As I mentioned in an earlier chapter, the clue is in the name!

Hose pipe – I have had mine for nearly 30 years and with the help of a spooling device to wind the pipe onto, has given good service in the garden and for other domestic jobs. With two outside taps, I use the same attachment for ease on both – Hozelock, in all its variants, is amongst the best but beware of all those hidden 'essential' extras that you might be tempted to buy. Computerised irrigation systems for when you are away on holiday – come back to a flooded garden or dried out pots because the micro-chip failed to perform!! There is no substitute for a good neighbour and a box of chocolates or a decent bottle of wine, plus the offer of doing the same for them when they are away is worth its weight in gold. They might even harvest some of your fruit and veg whilst you are away.

Kneeler – we have a plastic version that can act as a seat (with a small tool box in the lid) or as a kneeler with handles to help us get up and down – essential as one gets older.

Lawn mower – like many people, I have had and operated a number of different versions of these cursed contraptions over the years, both in my professional life and as an amateur gardener but, one rule always applies. A good quality mower can make a bad lawn look good but a poor quality mower will make a good quality lawn look bad. A cylinder mower with a decent, heavy rear roller produces the best finish of all, whether engine driven or electrical. Learn how to set the height of cut so that you do not scalp the lawn once a week - it only makes the grass grow faster, wears out some of the working parts and increases the amount of grass clippings that you have to dispose of! I now use a simple electric powered rotary mower set at its highest setting to avoid too much damage to any wildflowers that may have taken up residence in the lawn. I only cut my lawns every 2 – 3 weeks to allow my wildflowers to flower and benefit any creature that wishes to visit them – daisies, plantains, dandelions, hawkbits, clover and bugle, to name but a few. In the drought of the 2018 summer, I left the 'lawn' for more than a month.

Edging shears - although some people use strimmers to do this routine garden task, I prefer to old-fashioned technique!

My garden shed!

My border fork can be used as a garden rake as well for seed-bed preparation.

My trusty fork and trowel.

Two knives that I use on a regular basis in the garden.

Light and easy to handle small hand shears.

Light box – for those of us without glasshouse or conservatory space, the germination, rooting and growing on of young plants, particularly in the early part of the growing season, can be a nightmare. Etiolated seedlings never quite make the grade. Well, thanks to the late Geoff Hamilton's wonderful idea of a 'light box', you can grow sturdy seedlings and root lots of cuttings using this simple idea. A diagonally cut cardboard box, lined with silver foil and placed on a windowsill.

Potting bench – if like me you do not have a glasshouse and the kitchen worktop is 'out-of-bounds' then a mobile potting bench might be a useful addition to your gadget list. They are excellent for potting, propagation, pricking out, seed sowing etc.

Rain butt – attached to a downfall pipe from the house roof, this is essential for anyone trying to save water and money, has become an important part of my garden over the last 30 years or so. Just remember that rain water is cold so do not water house plants with it directly but fill a small watering can and bring it indoors to temper - as the water is soft (acidic), it is better for orchids and Gardenias. Do not use the rain water to water trays of young seedlings as the water may contain the fungal spores of various damping off diseases. Keep a lid on the rain butt to help reduce the chances of this happening. Keep two or three large pieces of charcoal in the butt to help soak up some of the nutrients and prevent it from turning into an algal soup. Empty and clean out the butt every spring time.

Saws – from the clumsy and poorly designed bow saws of my early career, I progressed to the modern folding pruning s aw that has become so popular and, as a working tool is more efficient and much safer. Felco's version is excellent and has done me proud over the last 10 years or so. The blades are replaceable.

Secateurs – for professional horticulturists there is only one manufacturer worthy of making and selling these essential garden tools – Felco – more expensive than the others but for a good reason! When properly sharpened, they can be used to take cuttings as well as doing their normal work of pruning. There are one or two modern designs with a ratchet operation that are excellent for those with difficulties with their wrists.

Sharpener – a sharpening device is essential for knives and secateurs and, although I do still have an old-fashioned carborundum sharpening stone, thesedays I much prefer the folding diamond blades.

Sickle – a small hand scythe that was the predecessor of the strimmer for longer grass – I use mine to trim under my hedge twice a year.

Another example of looking out for good quality products that will last you, as mine has.

Lots of variations now exist on this idea – a reversible stool with kneeler and small box for hand tools.

Rotary mowers are reasonably priced and easy to use, with a 'dead-man's handle' for safety.

Light box for those with only a windowsill to get young plants underway.

Mobile potting benches are another modern invention to make our gardening lives a little easier.

Folding saws are now 'the norm'.

Spade – I have one spade that has been with me for nearly 35 years and, although its blade is now about half its original length on account of the stony, sandy soil in our garden, it fits my left hand like a glove and has been known to move small mountains, with a little help from its operator. Spend a little more on a good spade and it will last you for most of your gardening life.

Springbok rake – like a giant back scratcher, this weapon gives me some good, strenuous exercise when I can be bothered to scarify the lawns but it is also the best tool for raking up rubbish, hedge trimmings, leaves and other detritus.

Step ladders – my own have been with me for over 35 years and can be adapted to a short 3 metre ladder as well as a pair of steps. I have a pair of extendable ladders for higher reach around the house if I need them but the steps cover the vast majority of tasks, both indoors and outdoors.

Strimmer – one of the curses of our modern age, spraying grass, soil, stones and other garden detritus everywhere. I have a battery operated one that is used very occasionally for those annoying bits of grass or for time saving, until you realise that it takes you longer to clear up the mess, that it has sprayed 10 metres from its starting point than it would have take you to do the job with hand tools. Operators of industrial strimmers have a lot of safe operator training and yet in our amateur gardens we receive no training at all.

Trug basket – it might make me sound like Miss Marple but I find it a good addition to my tool kit as it stops me from losing the other implements as I work around the garden.

Twine – although there are hundreds, if not thousands, of tying and securing devices on the market these days, a good ball of natural or green garden twine still provides the cheapest, easiest material for tying up plants and is a natural, renewable, biodegradable material.

Watering can – with a rain butt and a bird bath, I cannot survive without this garden essential – hanging baskets and such like are positioned at a height that stops the need for buying all those attachments and extenders for the hose pipe and saves you water at the same time.

Weather vane – given to me by a group of adult students when I finished working at the local technical college, this, along with my electronic weather station, provides me with a daily guide as to what the weather is doing or might be doing in a few hours time. The symbol on the top of the vane, made by a local blacksmith, is a capped gardener clipping a piece of containerised topiary! See Chapter Three for more on this essential subject for all gardeners. In addition,

Secateurs: easy to use and easy to clean. Worth those few extra £s.

The new generation of folding sharpeners are excellent for more than just garden tools.

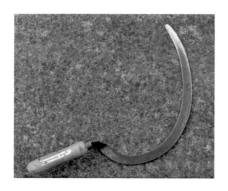

Sickle: very handy, very quiet but needs practice to get it to do its job.

You can even see my left-handed bias on the wear on the blade.

The biggest back scratcher on the planet!

Very flexible item to have.

I also have one of those electronic weather stations that helps me to monitor a variety of weather phenomenon.

Wheelbarrow – a cheap but long-lasting builders wheelbarrow that is often borrowed, or should that be barrowed, by neighbours. It has been with me since our move to Huddersfield in 1984 and shows no signs of giving up the ghost. I have only replaced the inner-tube once in all that time. I foolishly purchased a 'ball barrow' when we lived in Nottingham – a clever marketing ploy sucked me in and spat me out with my wallet slightly lighter!

Trug: I consider this to be a garden essential.

Never be without a ball of twine.

My old-fashioned style weather vane and its modern electronic equivalent help me to keep an eye on wind direction and speed.

Cheap as chips from a builder's merchants.

Chapter Nine

Bugs, Beasties and Other Nasties

I am fonder of my garden for all the trouble it gives me.

Reginald Farrer (1880–1920)
From: My Rock-Garden (1907)

IT HAS BEEN said that, if the human race were to die out now, the rest of the living world would continue to survive and in fact probably go on to thrive in numbers and variety not seen since the human race made its first attempts to control it some 10,000 years ago. It is also suggested that if the insect world were to die out now, the human race would disappear within 2 years. Whether these scare-mongering ideas would ever occur, it would certainly put the human race back in its place, not as the dominant and very superior species that it thinks it is, but as just another species of living organism that must learn to live with all other earthly inhabitants in harmony and balance if it is to survive.

Since the human race made its first tentative steps into the modern world and started to take control over plants and animals for its own benefit, the alternative and often unseen world of pests, weeds and diseases has been pulling in the opposite direction, attacking the crops and beasts at every given opportunity to satisfy their own need for procreation, sustenance and survival.

This battle has lead the human race, progressively, towards our current, unsustainable situation where the balance has been upset so much that, in some parts of the world, crop failure and destruction is causing humans to suffer and die.

Of course, in our own protected Western society, no such Doomsday scenario is likely to happen in the immediate future and, with environmental, ecological, social, economic and political pressures, we are thankfully beginning to change our thinking and our ways.

Part of this change is the acceptance that not all living creatures are going to destroy our crops and gardens and so blanket spraying of crops with pesticides which can kill out everything that moves is now much less common and the organic movement is gradually influencing all of us to consider the non-chemical alternatives to the more traditional ideas. What a shame that we went down that path in the first place. If you haven't read Rachel Carson's 'Silent Spring' I suggest that you find a copy and absorb the messages that she put into this valuable book - the beginnings of the modern organic movement. See the Bibiography for more details.

In this chapter, I have tried to give an outline of some of the major groups of pests and diseases, their strange ways and one or two hopefully useful ideas on how to manage them in a garden environment without wiping them off the face of the earth – after all, there are enough plants and creatures that are already extinct or are on some red list of endangered species, without our crude, inconsiderate efforts making things even worse.

Pests – what is a pest? I feel sure that we can all produce an extensive list of those creatures that have visited our gardens to take a quick meal from one of our favourite plants or have decided that our garden is a suitable place to mate and produce the next generation to devour our garden plants and crops. Whatever creatures are on that list, we must understand that they are just part of a complex food web that nature has developed and that we have disrupted.

The development of a relatively harmless, often tiny creature from insignificant wild insect to cultivated garden pest status is not the fault of the creature but of the grower. Our desire to grow plants from all over the globe has, in itself, given us more 'pests' than our island would naturally have and our strange desire for those 'must have' plants has helped to turn occasional nibblers into major 'pests.' The Scarlet Lily Beetle was almost unheard of in domestic gardening circles 20 years ago and yet now, our strange unwitting desire to grow *Liliums* in our gardens in every increasing numbers, particularly in containers, has caused this creature to take on Dracula like proportions. The omnipresent Vine Weevil was almost unheard of as a garden pest until the early 1970s. With the advent of garden centres and containerised plant production, the vine weevil found a new source of food for its larvae and gradually the vine weevil spread from nurseries to gardens where it now enjoys the perfect environment - lots of roots for its larvae, lots of thick, evergreen leaves for the adults and lots of plant debris to overwinter in – none of this caused by the vine weevil!!

As I wrote this piece originally in December 2012, the latest news was that a strain of Vinegar fly, *Drosophila suzukii* from the Far East, had finally hit our shores and now attacks soft and stone fruits in Kent, many of which are grown under polythene tunnels, erected to grow our early soft fruits and salad vegetables, that create the warm, humid conditions suited to this destructive fly. There are many more examples like this that have arrived on our shores over the last two hundred years or so since plant hunters and, more recently, tourists and importers have brought untold numbers and varieties of pests and diseases to our farms and gardens. Dutch Elm Disease, Ash Dieback, Flatworms, Asian Hornets etc, etc!

The following pages cover the major groups of pests, from large, four-legged, hairy ones to microscopic eight-legged ones, with some thoughts on ways in which we might begin to manage them more effectively than we have over the last 100 years or so.

INVERTEBRATES

Gastropods – The Slugs and Snails

With some 24 British species of slugs, you might expect a lot of damage on the garden plot. Wrong! There are only six species that are known to be very destructive in the garden, with the remaining 18 species eating fungi, decaying matter and earth worms (yes, some are carnivorous). Lift up the cover of your compost heap and you will find the Yellow Slug, *Limax flavus*, helping you to dispose of your garden waste (see Chapter 7 for an image of these), some of which might be plants destroyed by some of the slugs highlighted below. The small Netted or Grey Field Slug, *Deroceras reticulata,* with its fawn and white body, is probably one of the most destructive in our gardens. The tiny Common Garden Slug, *Arion hortensis,* with its dark brown or black body and a yellow sole enjoys seedlings, lettuces, strawberries and potato tubers. There are others, including the Black keeled slug, *Milax* spp that are a major problem on Potatoes and the Large Black Slug, *Arion ater.* And yet, when we apply the Metaldehyde based slug pellets, they do not distinguish the goodies from the badies. These randomly distributed blue pellets are linked with the killing off of the beneficial slugs as well as the natural predators such as Centipedes, Ground Beetles, Frogs, Hedgehogs and birds. With plenty of organic and non-chemical alternatives to choose from nowadays, including biological controlling nematodes, there is no need to use these outdated chemical controls any more – ask yourself why the slug problem seems to have got worse

The Large Black Slug, Arion ater, is one of the most destructive and is a polyphagous pest, eating almost any green plant material that it comes across.

over the last 30 years, since the advent of Metaldehyde! Read a fully story of these amazing and diverse molluscs in Michael Chinery's book, *The Natural History of the* Garden - see Bibliography for details.

Snails have, or seem to have, been on the increase over the last 10 years or so here in West Yorkshire, although I can remember them in the 1950s when I lived in Southend-on-Sea – maybe it has taken them that long to walk up the A1! With

The 'humbug snail,' Cepaea hortensis, is not a major pest but forms part of the rich tapestry of creatures that choose to call my home, whether as permanent residents or as transitory visitors.

over 200 species of land-based snails in Britain and Ireland, you might wonder that anything is left for us to grow, let alone eat or enjoy. That is, of course, after the slugs have had their fill. The Common Garden Snail, *Helix aspersa*, is the one that most of us have experience of, although occasionally, you might be lucky enough to see *Cepaea hortensis*, the white-lipped banded snail, more commonly known as the humbug snail – it appeared in my garden for the first time, as far as I know, about 10 years ago. To get more out this fascinating and sometimes devastating creature, why not visit the www.field-studies-council.org website and treat yourself to the latest version of the Land Snails in the British Isles (2nd Edition) chart, by Robert Cameron and Gordon Riley.

The management of these Gastropods in our garden environments has caused more questions than any other garden pest for me and probably every other professional garden advisor over the last twenty years or so and two of the best publications to hit the bookshelves in recent years, giving us lots of alternative methods to consider, beyond the Metaldehyde one are: *The Little Book of Slugs*, edited by Allan Shepherd and Suzanne Galant, published by the Centre for Alternative Technology in 2002; *50 Ways to Kill a Slug* by Sarah Ford – both of these are written a little tongue-in-cheek but do contain some interesting ideas that you might wish to try out.

The two most successful methods of reducing these sluggish but devastating creatures are: Hand picking of adults at dusk as soon as you see them in spring so that you can break the breeding cycle, choosing whichever method you like to dispose of them; tracing the adults back to their diurnal resting place in the morning, using the slime trails to track them, and gathering up handfuls of snail families. On wet days they will work all day long, giving you another opportunity to gather them up. In dry periods of weather, try watering in the morning as this is not only better for the plants but does not leave a scented water trail at night for slugs and snails to follow. Check out your local garden centre for organic alternatives to Metaldehyde – there are now plenty to choose from.

HYMENOPTERA

Formicoidae – The Family of Ants. Myrmecology – The Study of Ants

Visit a garden centre and scan the shelves for chemicals designed to rid your garden of ants. A whole plethora of products are there to help you destroy one of the most beneficial creatures in our gardens. Yes, one or two will give you a nip if you happen to sit on an unsuspecting ant's nest whilst enjoying a

The black ant, Lasius niger, is seen here feeding on the honeydew exuded by one of the Blackcurrant aphids, Cryptomyzus geleopsidis. They protect the aphids from parasitic and predatory creatures.

picnic or barbeque in the garden with family and friends, but remember that all they are after is some of the sugar that your food contains and you have got in their way – who is at fault? With more than 60 species of ants, native and non-native, in the UK and more than 11,000 species worldwide, you can imagine that none of us is ever very far from an ant's nest. Thus, despite all these products, designed to control ants in our gardens, the ant populations are alive, well and thriving. Ask anyone living in or around Easingwold – known locally as the ant capital of Yorkshire!

So why, as gardeners, should we be caring for or killing these industrious creatures? For my part, I do not have a problem with them, other than that some species that 'milk' aphids actually move aphids to the most succulent parts of plants so that the amount of honeydew excreted by the aphids is increased and so that amount of sugary sap is increased for the ants to consume. It is for this reason that we sometimes find ants coming into our houses, as they search out sources of sugar – if you are a messy cook or are a little clumsy when you add sugar to hot drinks, the spilt sugar becomes the attraction for ants – when one worker ant finds it, the message goes back to the nest and their fellow ants come back for more. These same ants may also help to maintain a high aphid population by killing off parasitic and predatory insects – the negative side of the ant equation!

What else do they feed on? As many ant species are omnivorous and opportunist, it is difficult to list their food supplies but, suffice it to say that your garden would have a lot more debris and micro-insects if it was not for ants. Also remember that in the often complex food webs of our gardens, the ants become a source of food for other creatures, including insect eating birds such as Blackbirds.

One of the main species that we find in our gardens is *Lasius niger*, the common black garden ant, that can be found on the edges of lawns and under paving slabs. It has no sting but will bite if given provocation as well as squirting formic acid at the offending object. Colonies can reach up to 15,000 in a good season. One of the red ants, *Myrmica rubra*, can give a very painful sting if disturbed but tends to live in smaller colonies of around 200 – I experienced the bite of these red devils whilst kneeling on my lawn with my grandchildren, shelling peas!

So, think twice before you slosh ant killers around your garden – in the longer term these random materials are unlikely to have much effect on the populations and you may regret their demise once they have gone.

Apocrita - Bees and wasps – this familiar group, that forms a major part of the Hymenoptera order, are amongst the most important of all the insects in our garden and we ignore them at our peril. Unfortunately, for most of us, our memory of bees and wasps is that they sting and that the sting hurts! The fact that around one third of all the food that we consume is there as a direct result of insect pollination work and that a vast number of the wasps that we have in our gardens are actually beneficial, predatory or parasitic insects, helping us to keep true garden pests under some level of control, are often ignored as we are chased around the garden by an infuriated wasp! Read through the various plant families in Appendix 1 to see if you have enough floral diversity to help support these vital creatures.

Bees (Apoidae) – these are roughly divided into two main groups:- communal bees that survive in large communal groups, commonly known as hives, and solitary bees that lay eggs singly, leaving any offspring to fend for themselves. As one of the major insect groups for pollination across the planet, it is surely our responsibility to help preserve and conserve these incredible creatures. Current estimates suggest that around one third of all the food that the human race consumes is directly linked to the pollination processes that bees undertake. Over recent years there has been much concern about the dramatic decline in the populations of honey bees and of a number of bumble bee species. Is it because of natural cycles of life or because of something that we humans have done? The jury still seems to be out on this and various bee organisations across the world are

Our common honey bee, Apis mellifera, seen here in a small swarm in my boundary hedge and also enjoying the flowers on the climbing Hydrangea, Hydrangea petiolaris, has been under threat in recent years for a number of reasons, including the use of neonicotinoid pesticides.

carrying out extensive research as well as putting pressure on governments to help us understand and resolve this potentially disastrous situation. Colony collapse disorder, Varroa mites, various viruses and the use of Neonicotinoid pesticides are just four possible causes for the decline, let alone the gradual and disastrous decline in flower rich meadows since the Second World War – North Yorkshire had some of the best of these and now has very few! It is now beholden on all those involved in all the land-based industries, both amateur and professional, to redress the balance and add the right type of floral diversity and volume to all land-based work that we do. For the bee population this includes using flowering trees, shrubs and herbaceous plants across all four seasons, less intrusive and intensive land management and ground cultivation techniques and a major reduction in the use of inorganic and organic pesticides, particularly during the height of the day when these creatures reach the zenith of their daily activities.

With over 20,000 known species of bees across the planet, and counting, the value of these often tiny creatures cannot be underestimated. The value of our social honey bees to us is legendary and we have taken advantage of their industrious nature for thousands of years. Flower pollination, honey and

The banded white-tailed bumblebee, Bombus lucorum, seen here climbing into the tempting tube of a foxglove, Digitalis purpurea, flower.

wax production are the more obvious ones but the health giving properties of honey, particularly the very expensive Manuka honey from New Zealand and the well-known antibacterial properties of honey are but a small fraction of the benefits that we can gain from honey bees.

Our own native bees, including the wonderful but aerodynamically disastrous banded, white-tailed Bumble bee, *Bombus lucorum*, are random feeders and so will wonder around your garden accidentally pollinating any flower that they visit. They often fly much earlier in the morning than honey bees and will continue late into the evening, long after the honey bees have returned to their hives.

Wasps (Vespoidea) – although we are all familiar with the wasps that annoy us in late summer, there are some other wasp species that are an important part of any eco-system – with an affective ovi-depositor for parasitic egg laying, the parasitic wasps now form an important part of the world's biological control, both naturally and artificially for agricultural and horticultural pests. The now well-known *Encarsia formosa* parasitic wasp has been used to help manage populations of the Glasshouse Whitefly for many years. Our own stinging wasp is one of the most affective predator on aphids but it is not that side of their lives that we normally observe.

LEPIDOPTERA

Butterflies

From 'The Butterfly' by Edmund Spenser (1552–1599).

> He the gay garden round about doth fly,
> From bed to bed, from one to other border,
> And takes survey with curious busy eye
> Of every flower and herb there set in order;
> Now this, now that, he tasteth tenderly,
> Ye none of them he rudely doth disorder,
> Ne with his feet their silken leaves deface,
> But pastures on the pleasures of each place.

Amongst the most beautiful creatures to visit our gardens from April to October, these flitting transitory adults are but a moment in time. However, it is not these mating machines that we need to understand, although some of them will benefit

The Large Cabbage White Butterfly, Pieris brassicae, seen here feeding on the flowers of Lavendula angustifolia, is one of the oliphagous pests seen in our gardens throughout late spring and summer.

from our support, with food sources such as Buddleia flowers. It is the eggs and caterpillars that should be our concern. Firstly, for any pest species such as the Large Cabbage White Butterfly, we need to know its lifecycle and its timing as well as being able to recognise the clusters of yellow eggs on the undersides of leaves and the multi-coloured caterpillars that like Brassicas for breakfast, lunch, afternoon tea, dinner and supper. For those butterflies that are not normally classified as garden pests such as the Holly Blue and the Orange tip butterflies, our concern should be, once again, for the eggs and caterpillars. This time however, it is our responsibility to help provide the all-important food plants that those beautiful adults will be searching for as they flit across our gardens - it is on these that they will lay their all-important eggs. Search out a copy of the Collins Field Guide to Caterpillars of Butterflies and Moths in Britain and Europe to help you unravel this mystery and read through Appendix 1 for examples of groups of plants that can support particular species of butterflies.

Moths - with more than 2300 different moths inhabiting our islands, you might imagine that there are some very beautiful ones, some rather ugly ones

The brightly coloured caterpillar of the Cinnabar Moth, Tyria jacobaeae, feeding on the foliage of Senecio jacobae.

and some that have your garden plants in their sights for a crafty meal or two. Like their butterfly relatives, moths have two sides to their lives - they can be a garden pest, as with Winter and Codling moths that attack our fruit trees or stunningly beautiful ones such as the Cinnabar moth that feeds on *Senecio jacobae* (Ragwort). One of the other strange facts about moths is that they can be diurnal, although the vast majority are nocturnal. Like butterflies, each species has a single plant or a group of plants that it needs to complete its life-cycle. The latest example to find my garden attractive is the Mint moth that feeds on a variety of Laminaceae herbs such as *Mentha* and *Thymus*.

HEMIPTERA

Aphids - the plague of British gardens and farms. With more than 500 species in Britain, you can be certain that at one time or another, regardless of season, there will be a representative from the aphid community in your garden, either as an egg, nymph, pedestrian or winged adult. Because most aphid reproduction is asexual, at least during the spring and summer months, this gives the females the potential to develop huge populations in a very short time, when feeding opportunities are at their best and we see the results of this on fruit trees, *Rosa* spps, beans, *Lupinus* and many other garden plants. If the mathematical calculations of potential population numbers were ever to be realised, we would all disappear under a very large heap of aphids. This has not and never will happen because of the huge number of factors that control these latent spring and summer explosions in numbers:- cool weather, rain, natural death, parasitic wasps and fungi, predators such as wasps, hoverflies, ladybirds, lacewings and a wide variety of birds – these creatures rely on these feeding frenzies for survival and the only disadvantage is that birds may cause some transitory damage to foliage and flowers – a small price to pay. If you use insecticides, you are likely to kill out the vast majority of the insect parasites and predators but will only kill out around 50% of the aphids, either because your spraying was not very accurate or, more likely, the remaining 50% are nowadays fully resistant to many of these manufactured chemicals. The use of fatty acid contact sprays at dawn or dusk, directly onto the clusters of aphids, is the most effective control in a domestic garden but requires constant vigilance to be successful.

Nematodes – another example of the pluses and minuses presented to us by Mother Nature. There are a number of nematodes (eelworms) that can cause serious damage to some of our garden plants such as the stem eelworm on the herbaceous *Phlox paniculata* but there are also nematodes that are proving to be very effective biological control organisms for slugs and several other garden pests. The pest species include other stem eelworms that can devastate *Narcissi*, *Alliums* and *Tulipas* and potatoes can be attacked by the potato cyst eelworm and the potato tuber eelworm which can move to other plants such as bulbous *Irises* and *Dahlias*. The *Chrysanthemum* eelworm is known to attack upwards of 150 different species of plants and has a widespread distribution, making it almost impossible to avoid in any normal garden. Symptoms are many and varied but include dark areas between the veins of leaves, flower bud distortion and general lack of vigour. Place a small piece of possible infected plant material in a glass jar of water for 30 minutes to see if a wriggling mass of eelworms appears – if so, destroy the plant. *Fragaria* spps (Strawberries) are amongst the commonest of plants to be attacked, with leaf crumpling and distortion being the commonest symptoms in spring and autumn – immersion in hot water (46°C) for 30 minutes is said to be an effective control but good hygiene and destruction of any infected stock is probably the best control. Root-knot eelworms can attack over 800 different plant species and, unless you are prepared to inspect the roots of all plants that you purchase, you are unlikely to know whether you are importing infected stock into your garden.

On the positive side of this equation, the last 20 years or so have seen a huge increase in the isolation and commercial development of species of eelworms that parasitize some of our garden pests, including leatherjackets, chafer grubs, slugs and vine weevil. This development is still going on and we are likely to see more pests being controlled by them as time goes on as we search for alternatives to pesticides for the management of our garden pests.

COLEOPTERA

Beetles – with over 400,000 (one fifth of the worlds known living organisms!) species known so far across the planet and some 5,000 present in Britain, you can be sure that amongst them, some will be classified by us as pests and some will be seen as beneficial insects. Like all forms of life on this planet, there are good ones and bad ones, ones that are native to our Islands and ones that have been imported from far off lands.

I have selected one or two of the more important ones for you to consider but I suggest that you visit the Royal Entomological Society website for a more details look at some of these goodies and badies.

Dung beetles are an essential part of the management of any grassland habitat and, with tunnellers, dwellers and rollers, there are enough of them across the planet to ensure that pastures and prairies do not get buried in animal droppings – their life processes help to recycle the materials and minerals in the droppings. Our own ground beetle, so common in many gardens and often found hiding under stones, is a powerful predator and, with over 300 species across the UK, you will have them in your garden! The larvae and adults are both carnivorous and can predate on slugs and snails. Being nocturnal, they need a protective hideaway for their diurnal rest and log or stone piles are amongst the best. Ladybirds come in all sizes and colours but one thing is certain – they are all veracious predators, both a larvae and adults on smaller creatures such as aphids and scale insects, giving us one of the best natural predators. Unfortunately, their populations tend to fluctuate widely and they are prone to being killed by inorganic pesticides being used during the height of the day when they are feeding most. Since 2004 they have also been attacked by the Harlequin Ladybird, an Asian species that has helped to reduce the UK population of 42 different species by some 40%. In addition, a parasitic wasp has been attacking our ladybirds since the late 1990s. The complexity of nature never ceases to amaze me.

Pest species that we need to be aware of include Chafer beetles, Vine Weevils, Scarlet Lily Beetles, Flea beetles, Raspberry beetles, Rosemary beetles, Wireworms (Click beetles) and Pea and bean weevils, although there are many more waiting in the wings to select a juicy asparagus spear, a Viburnum leaf or a succulent strawberry. A recent foreign invader is the Asian Longhorn beetle, (*Anoplophora glabripennis*) that is attacking a wide range of tree species!

Chafer beetles can attack below ground as a larvae and above ground as an adult, giving us similar symptoms to the ubiquitous vine weevil, although the larvae is larger and white, with three pairs of thoracic legs. It feeds on tubers, roots, corms and a range of common fruit, vegetables and ornamental garden plants and can be a major pest of lawns where damage is not only caused by the subterranean larvae but by predatory birds searching out a tasty meal. There are six different species of this pest.

The Vine Weevil has been a major pest in the horticultural industry for more than 40 years, being a polyphagous pest and is now widespread and endemic across the whole of the British Isles. In containers its grubs thrive on

The Rosemary beetle, Chrysolina americana actually originates from southern Europe and has been in the UK since the mid 1990s. It attacks Lavendula, Rosmarinus, Salvia and Thymus from August through to April but is present as an adult all year round.

succulent roots, causing plants to collapse or defoliate and, in the open garden the nocturnal adult causes visual devastation to many thick leaved evergreens. Controls nowadays include pesticides, nematodes for the grubs and a recently isolated parasitic fungus called *Beauveria bassiana* to control the adult (not currently available in the UK), although squashology is still helpful in reducing the breeding cycle of this destructive garden pest.

Lumbricidae - Earthworms - with an estimated 3000 species of them worldwide and at least 25 species identified in the UK, these rather strange, hermaphrodite invertebrates punch well above their individual weight in our gardens and across the wider landscape. Charles Darwin described them as 'nature's ploughs' and that is what they do for the vast majority of their lives, eating soil and organic matter and excreting the remains to help create healthy, friable soil for plants. Their work assists bacteria and fungi to process animal and plant waste so that the minerals can be recycled for animals and plants to benefit from – the perfect natural cycle.

In our borders and lawns we might find *Lumbricus terrestris*, the lob worm or *Allolobophora chlorotica,* the green earthworm, working their magic and helping our soil to stay healthy, with up to 40 per square metre – of course, in turn, they become food for hungry blackbirds and thrushes and they also bring their faeces to the surface in spring and autumn, giving us the unsightly worm casts that so annoy gardeners who love their lawns. The processed soil and organic matter is full of goodness and, once the casts have been re-distributed across your lawn by a brush, a mower or the rain, this goodness helps your lawn to thrive. The tunnels made by the worms, that can be up to 1 metre deep or more, act as drainage channels, taking surplus water away from the surface and helping to reduce the growth of moss and dog lichen. To think that 25 years ago we had access to chemicals to kill off these vital creatures!

Be aware that two earthworm predators, the Australian and New Zealand flatworms are active in some northern parts of the UK and Ireland and are a threat to our native earthworms!

In our compost heaps, more of which later in this chapter, the brandling worm, *Eisenia fetida*, is one of the most remarkable creatures, processing vast quantities of garden waste for us in another of those essential symbiotic relationships. Given the right environment that is neutral to alkaline, warm and moist, it and thousands of relatives will help to process green kitchen waste and garden waste into brown gold within a matter of months that we can reuse in our gardens as free planting compost.

For more information on these important garden creatures why not visit www.earthwormsoc.org.uk, the web site of the Earthworm Society of Britain.

Vertebrates

Amphibians – frogs, newts and toads should form an important part of the biodiversity of all our gardens as their contribution to the management of pests such as slugs is way beyond their size and number. Since World War Two farm ponds and ditches have been drained or filled in, taking many of the semi-natural environments of these creatures away and the garden pond has become an essential substitute to allow them to survive. So, if you are able to have a natural pond in your garden, without fish and electronics, you will be able to support a small population of some or all of them and, in return, they will not only give you pleasure as you observe their antics but they may help to reduce your slug and snail populations.

Mammals – like all groups of creatures on Mother Nature's earth, there are beneficial and detrimental examples within this complex world of internal skeletons, warm blood, live young and four limbs. For us humans, as examples of the mammalian group, our views on the goodies and baddies are as varied as the members of the group. Cuddly kitties, fluffy bunnies, cute squirrels and beautiful badgers are all part of the mix and it is for each of us to decide whether we see them as an important part of the biodiversity of our garden or a curse that we could really do without. As a simple example from my own tiny piece of the UK, I have a regular visit from a badger who insists on cultivating a deep hole in the back of one of my borders, up to 15cm deep, to use as a temporary toilet. Having filled one hole with what I now see as free fertilizer, he / she may choose to dig another or go elsewhere. In my compost heap, I have a resident family of field mice that use the shredded paper which I add from my domestic and business life, as part of the carbon / nitrogen mix as their nesting material and, of course, they consume apple cores and other vegetative biodegradable delicacies that we add to the compost heap from the kitchen. One mammal, or should I say, several mammals that I have as regular nocturnal visitors to the garden are the semi-domesticated felines from across our neighbourhood. I suppose it is an inevitable price that we have had to pay for supporting and attracting the wide variety of birds that choose our garden as a haven for shelter, food and nesting opportunities. The only issue that I have is that is that the birds are outnumbered as compared with truly wild circumstances where there might be one wild cat per

Our common frog, Rana temporaria, is one of the most common amphibians that we will see and hear during our lives in the UK.

The European badger, Meles meles, caught here on my wildlife camera, is now a regular visitor to our garden, usually whilst I am in the land of dreams.

Our 'resident' noisy male blackbird, Turdus merula, perched happily on the roof of the garden shed.

square kilometre. If you are a cat owner / lover, please hang a bell around its neck so that the birds can hear the cat before it pounces, not afterwards! Over recent years, we have been treated to a visit by a mole – quite where this half-blind subterranean worm eater has come from, I do not know but, on the positive side, it is a good indicator of a healthy earthworm population. Unfortunately for us, it is making a mess in the small area of 'woodland' at the bottom of the garden, dislodging bulbs, tree roots and woodland herbaceous plants as it chases up and down its tunnels. Unfortunately for the mole, I have access to a mole trap! I have had a new visitor recently in the form of a hedgehog – not seen but his / her deposits are very recognisable! An occasional covered dish of dog food seems to be emptied overnight and, I assume that he/she is also devouring a few slugs and snails as well.

The only flying mammals to visit our garden are the bats in summer and I have not been able to identify which species they are. However, their nightly swooping and soaring around our garden seems to suggest that they are finding sufficient food in the form of flies and moths, some of which will be unwanted garden pests and this in turn suggests that there is a lot of flying biodiversity in my garden for them enjoy.

Each of these examples, and perhaps other unseen ones, is an integral part of the complex food web that has formed over the 30+ years that my garden has evolved, let alone the millennia that passed before the house was built. I put shredded business and personal papers onto my compost occasionally and have recently discovered that a family of field mice seem to enjoy the nesting material as well as nibbling on some of the kitchen green waste that I add to the heap. Whether these attract our feline 'friends' I do not know but the mice seem to be a permanent feature of the garden now. We also have suburban foxes visiting the garden and one of their favourite pastimes seems to be digging small holes in the 'lawn', presumably in search of a juicy worm – this may be another indicator of a healthy worm population and, as I am not precious about my lawn from a visual sense, a few tiny holes is a small price to pay.

So, apart from the disproportionate number of domestic cats in our area, the other mammalian visitors can either be tolerated or enjoyed, depending on how you see these wild creatures. Because of the open boundaries (hedges and open fences) on two sides of my garden, they are able to come and go as they please.

Birds – the Avifauna or Aves, depending on which book you read, are an integral part of the life of our gardens, not to be ignored. With nearly 600 species of birds recorded as either living in or visiting the UK up to the end of 2011, divided into a number of distinct groups, there is a good chance that your garden will have at least 10 species leaving their calling card over a twelve month period, if not more. In my own garden, taken from my un-scientific observation records over a 12 year period, from 1986 until 1998, I observed more than 30 species of birds using my garden as a resting, feeding, sheltering or breeding site. I wonder how many more I missed whilst I was otherwise occupied with work, family or vacations.

The large majority of our 'garden birds' are known as passerines or perching birds but we can also have occasional visits from game birds and other non-passerines, wading birds, waterfowl, seabirds, owls and birds of prey, all of which will choose to visit our small pieces of Britain for their own peculiar reasons. Take a look at the RSPB Pocket Birds of Britain and Europe for more on how the bird world is sub-divided.

If you look at the positive side of birds in our gardens, the list of benefits far outweighs any negative issues. Free fertiliser, in the form of guano, almost every time they visit, sometimes loaded with free seeds that you may or may not want. The visual benefits for us as we observe a blackbird heaving on an earth worm in the lawn, a song thrush cracking open a snail on a stone or a group of hungry sparrows leaping up to grab an aphid from the leaves of a tree - positive symbiotic relationships for both birds and humans, without either one having anything to do with the other, directly.

Of course, for every positive action there is an equal and opposite reaction, so Sir Isaac Newton's 3rd Law states. Get a beautiful blackbird to visit or stay in your garden, giving you that wonderful dawn chorus from 4 am in the morning and you can bet that, if you don't protect your soft fruit, the blackbird will have had a very juicy breakfast before you have arisen from your disturbed slumbers. With a little effort and a small investment you can stop his or her antics without having to get out of bed.

To give you an idea of some of the wonderful and terrible activities that I have observed, I have listed a selection of them below. Add your own to the list as you see them.

a. Goldfinches drinking from the cups formed in the leaf joints of Teasels in mid-summer.

b. Magpies stripping out eggs and hatchlings from a robin's nest!

c. Blackbirds harvesting ants from a nest on the edge of the lawn.

d. Herons picking out frogs from the pond.

e. Long-tailed tits hanging upside down on a *Prunus padus*, feeding on aphid eggs in winter and the adults in spring.

f. Swifts swooping across the garden harvesting aphids as they fly.

g. Bullfinches nipping out succulent fruit buds from the apple trees as they swell in early spring.

h. A speedy sparrow hawk snatching an unsuspecting sparrow from the top of the hedge.

i. A family of blue tits scurrying around the branches of an apple tree in the middle of winter in search of an odd aphid or winter moth egg.

j. A local large ginger tomcat dragging an uncooperative magpie back home to show to its owners.

One last note on the story of our garden birds – to feed or not to feed, that is the question. With every newspaper and news item on radio and TV giving us more horror stories about the decline of yet another species of bird, we need to ask the question about the value and purpose of feeding garden birds over the last 20 years or so. Every garden centre, general shop and market stall is selling us an ever wider and more expensive variety of sizes and shapes of feeders to hang in our gardens and every variation on the word bird food is sold to us at ever-increasing prices to encourage us to believe that, by providing the local robin population with dried mealworms or the finch population with its own special mixture of seeds, we are doing our bit to support the ornithological health and diversity of our nation. Up until the early part of the 21st century the RSPB and other eminent organisations were telling us to avoid feeding during the nesting season so that fledgling birds did not choke on pieces of peanuts and other seed-based foods. Now we are told that we should feed all year round to ensure that birds get continuity of supply. My own opinion is that the whole bird food industry is profit led and has little to do with supporting and stimulating the dwindling bird population and that we should provide garden environments that encourage creature diversity and complex food webs that naturally support birds, giving them the opportunity to feed according to their instincts rather than surviving by the greedy feeding frenzies that we see on our bird feeders, many of which are sources of disease!

Diseases

The study of diseases is classified as pathology, although this can conjure up images of laboratories full of microscopes and scientists in white coats. From the horticultural perspective, diseases are classified under three headings: fungi, bacteria and viruses. Each of these, with their microscopic makeup and complex life processes, can cause devastation to our garden plants and crops. However, if you look on the other side of the fence, many of them are involved in supporting and protecting our plants from the ravages of other diseases and pests, giving us the chance to use them for the good of our precious plants.

These complex relationships between plants and other living organisms take another twist when you find out that some plants can act as alternative hosts for some diseases without us being aware of it - the reverse of companion planting: e.g. If I allow *Trifolium repens* (clover) to grow in my lawn, which I do, and I grow *Lathyrus odoratus* (Sweet Pea) in my garden, which I do sometimes, there is a possibility that, with the help of a sap-sucking aphid, the Pea Enation Mosaic Virus may be transferred from the clover, that carries the virus but shows no symptoms, to the sweet pea, where the symptoms are devastating, if not fatal. There are many more examples of these complex and often hidden relationships that we need to discover to help reduce the incidence of diseases in our gardens, let alone the wider world.

In the human world, because of our complex genetic make-up, each of us has various levels of susceptibility and resistance to the diseases that can attack us. In the plant world exactly the same is true – over the years of human intervention in the plant world, cultivars of flowers, fruit and vegetables have been discovered and isolated that have known resistance to particular diseases, giving us another chance to avoid the use of inorganic pesticides to 'control' these problems. In recent years, as our scientific knowledge has developed, we now know that the diseases that attack plants, let alone the ones that attack humans, can evolve very quickly and any apparent resistance to a disease that a plant has been shown to have may break down with the new strain of disease!

Fungi – of all the organisms that have evolved on this planet over the last 3.5 billion years, the world of fungi must be one of the most complex and diverse. Without these remarkable organisms and a few trillion bacteria, the world would have been buried in its own waste by the time the dinosaurs arrived. Like all groups of organisms, fungi have evolved beneficial and detrimental variations to challenge us, whether they are in our gardens, our homes or our work. Examples that challenge us include bread moulds, dry rot of timber, damp moulds on house walls and damping off of our precious seedlings. Of course, on the positive side of that equation, we all enjoy mushrooms to eat and many of us have had a penicillin injection to kill off a bacterial infection!

These complex organisms have many strange phases to their lives to help ensure that they can survive when food supplies are not available, as well as when they are plentiful. Spores released in their trillions from fungal fruiting bodies are the most obvious, as you might have observed if you have ever trodden on a ripe puff ball, and it is these that get blown around on air currents, washed down water courses and transferred on our clothes, shoes, tools and in our compost – the atmosphere contains trillions of them and it only when the conditions are right that they can begin their work. The recent invasion of *Hymenoscyphus fraxineus* (Ash dieback disease) from Europe that is now attacking the *Fraxinus excelsior* stock in the UK is a prime example of a fungus whose spores can be transferred on the wind as well as on infected plants. Beyond these most obvious methods of spread, fungi can survive as microscopic desiccated organisms for years in soil, only to rear their ugly heads when we plant the next host crop. The devastating *Brassica* disease, club root, can survive in the garden soil for upwards of twenty years, leaving those gardeners with infected soil little chance of being able to grow *Brassica* successfully, unless of course they grow one of the new generation of reportedly resistant cultivars!

Because of how the fungi work when they are active, the effects we see are often collapsed and sunken leaf, stem, flower and root tissue. This is because the fungus works unseen below the surface of the plant, dissolving the tissue with the aid of complex enzymes and it is not until the fungus has done its dirty work that we see a fruiting body emerging above the surface – as obvious examples, mould infected bread can be tasted before we see the grey mould on the surface of the slice and mushrooms have to develop their mycelium for some weeks under the surface of a pile of horse manure before we see the edible mushrooms on the surface.

For us to manage the complexity of this pathological world, we must try to focus on the most prevalent fungal diseases and try to understand them. Take a simple and common example that every gardener will have present in their gardens at one time or another. The disease, *Botrytis cinerea* (Grey Mould), is one of the curses of gardening, with its ability to attack flower buds and rot succulent strawberries after a thunderstorm, collapse a lettuce crop in a matter of days if we overdo the watering and attack our favourite house plant whilst we are away on holiday. Control, in its purest sense, is impossible but reduction and prevention can be achieved by 'good gardening.' The fungus thrives in cool, damp, stagnant conditions as many, but not all, fungi do. For us gardeners this means good spacing of plants in glasshouses, avoidance of evening

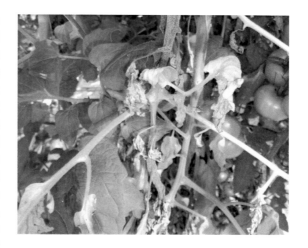

Botrytis cinerea in all its glory on a tomato leaf. Physical damage, cool nights and high humidity in the right combination will almost certainly wake this fungal disease up.

watering and removal of any dead and dying flowers and foliage that may act as a starting point for the fungus – good examples of cultural control.

On a more positive note, the fungus is used by some viticulturists to create the distinctive Sauterne wines as the bunches of grapes are actually 'left to rot' on the vine, with *Botrytis cinerea* acting as the rotting agent. To add to the positive, there is a parasitic fungus called *Gliocladium roseum* that attacks *Botrytis cinerea* – the power, balance and diversity of nature.

Fungal diseases to be aware of include: Potato and tomato blight, Clubroot, Powdery mildew, Downy mildew, Rose blackspot and Honey fungus.

Bacteria – although certain bacteria can cause seriously disfiguring symptoms on our precious plants, the vast majority of bacteria are harmless or beneficial to us and our gardens and so, if you are in any way negative about these microscopic organisms, now is the opportunity to change your mind.

Consider the contents of our stomachs as a good starting point that we can all relate to! Without a variety of good bacteria and the enzymes that work alongside them, we would not be able to process the food that we eat and benefit from. Of course, there are occasions, after eating some poorly prepared food, that bad bacterium can get into our systems and cause a temporary upset and we, as careful and caring human beings, should always try to avoid these situations for ourselves and our loved ones. From a purely environmental point of view, Methane gas is one of the worst greenhouse gases and it is produced by anaerobic bacteria in the stomachs of carnivores and omnivores! Having said that, the new anaerobic bio-digesters that are being used by the commercial horticulture industry to produce Methane gas for heating glasshouses prove that, once you know the science, you can turn it to your advantage. For anyone who has a septic tank within their property, you should know that the decomposition of your family's waste is done by bacteria – put anything too poisonous down your drains or toilets and you may find that your septic tank stops working properly!

The air that we breathe is, for the most part, Nitrogen gas and there are a number of specialist bacteria that can extract this gas from the air and store it in the roots of certain plants. This fantastic symbiotic relationship between the plants and the bacteria provides us with a free, environmentally friendly and continuous supply of Nitrogen for our plants. Plants in the Leguminosae family are amongst the best examples and form an important part of the crop rotation cycle where we can grow leafy salad and Brassica crops on land that has been used for peas and beans in the previous growing season so that they can take advantage of the free Nitrogen source. *Alnus* is one of the oddities of the plant world that can also have this symbiotic relationship with bacteria. To add to this incredible natural process, scientists have been researching the possibility, through the modern concept of Genetic Modification (GM), of extracting the gene that allows bacteria and Legumes to fix Nitrogen on the roots of Leguminosae plants and 'transplant' it into the DNA of cereal crops. This would help developing countries to feed themselves, without the need for expensive Nitrogenous fertilizers. Just to clarify my position, I do not necessarily approve of GM as a modern science because so much of it has not been done for the right reasons. However, the Genie is now out of the bottle!

In our ordinary garden soils it is estimated that upwards of 40 million bacteria live in just one gram of soil carrying out a variety of functions without us ever knowing about it. In well-drained healthy soils this population, alongside mycorrhiza and other fungal organisms, will help to ensure the health of your garden and our plants. In your compost heap, providing that it is aerobic, the bacteria will help to process your garden waste, along with all the other composting agents.

On the negative side of this bacterial equation, there are a number of diseases that we need to be aware of and alert to. It is important to remember that, if you discover any of these in your garden, you should not compost any of the infected plant material or move the material to another site but preferably burn it on your own site to avoid any cross-infection.

Bacterial diseases to be aware of include: Ash canker, Fire blight, Lilac blight, *Prunus* bacterial canker, Poplar bacterial canker and *Clematis* slime flux.

Viruses – of all the diseases that nature has designed to attack our precious plants, viruses are perhaps the most insidious. They seem to move, almost unseen by us, from plant to plant and garden to garden, using our garden tools, our hands and sap-sucking insects amongst other devious methods. What we see are distorted and discoloured leaves, flowers and fruits and, over time, stunted growth, perhaps even without realising that it is a virus that is causing the damage. In some plants the virus has produced effects that we like such as mottled flower petals or foliage with a mosaic pattern on it. In the commercial world of glasshouse grown salad crops such as tomatoes, peppers and cucumbers, it is a major problem and, in the world of plant sales, growing and selling certified stock it is very difficult to guarantee virus free stock.

Some 40 years ago, when micropropagation was in its infancy, a technique known as meristem culture was tested and, using the meristematic tissue at the very centre of a growth bud, that is virus free, plants were produced under protection that were free of any known viruses – in one example this produced Rhubarb stalks as thick as a man's leg. The suggestion is, perhaps, that many plants have viruses as a natural part of their makeup and it would be irresponsible of us to try and remove them, only for them to be re-infected once they get out into the great wide world.

Physiological disorders – of all the influences on our garden plants, the physiological disorders are amongst the hardest to manage. From sun scorch to wind damage and frost damage to nutrient deficiencies, these factors that can destroy flowers, foliage and roots often leave us frustrated and confused. Organic gardeners will spend half their gardening time using techniques to help reduce the likelihood of these external influences affecting their precious plants. I have listed some of the more commonly occurring disorders, with some indicators of what we can do to reduce their incidence:

1. **Blindness** – this may be a genetic defect but lack of flowering is often caused by the plant not receiving the necessary food, day length or light levels at the right stage of growth.

2. **CO² toxicity** – this usually occurs in heated glasshouses where gas heaters are used at night when the plants do not use CO_2 and additional ventilation is often all that is needed to rectify the problem.

3. **Drought** – the knock on effects of drought or even poor watering, whether temporary or prolonged, are many and varied and it requires vigilance on the part of the gardener to ensure that any one plant has the necessary available water at the right time of day, season or year to ensure its success. Poor foliage, flowering and fruiting are all symptoms of this, let alone the more immediate and obvious wilting.

4. **Etiolation** – the stretching of the internodes occurs when any one plant does not receive the right light levels for it to perform – woodland plants are genetically adapted to low light whereas most vegetables are not – right plant, right place and right spacing usually ensures that etiolation does not occur.

5. **Fasciation** – this strange flattening of the stems of some plants has no obvious cause and so affected plants are often best removed or the offending stem removed.

6. **Frost damage** – examples of frost damage on Camellia flowers and Hydrangea buds are amongst the more common and these can be prevented by correct location of plants and good growing techniques. Know your plant and its needs.

7. **Nutrient deficiencies** – like human beings, plants are very sensitive to shortages of the right foods and, the old saying 'you are what you eat' is as true in the plant world as it is in the human one. Poor flowering and fruiting of tomatoes can be due to a shortage of Potassium in the compost and small purple leaves on a Brassica plant can indicate shortage of Nitrogen.

8. **Nutrient toxicity** – do not kill your plants with kindness and you will avoid nutrient toxicity. Over liming of allotment soils can cause chlorosis (yellowing) of the leaves of vegetables and growing an acid loving plant in an alkaline soil can give the same effect.

9. **Oedema** – small droplets of water appearing on the surface of leaves is the typical symptom and this is oedema. *Impatiens* are commonly affected by this and it is caused by over-watering.

10. **Reversion** – green stems on variegated plants is the usual symptom of reversion. These need to be removed as soon as they are identified to prevent them from taking over the parent plant. We have all seen green patches in variegated hedges. Remember that variegated plants do not survive long in the wild as the plant naturally reverts back to its green parentage.

11. **Sun scorch** – right plant, right place is the usual way of preventing this from occurring as it is only plants that do not like excessively high light levels that are affected by this.

12. **Water logging** – with recent high rainfall across the UK, we are likely to see many plants suffering from this – it is often the collapse of the root system, through anaerobic soil conditions but this is sometimes followed by bacterial and fungal rots as secondary infections and these may well finish the plant off. This can occur in containers as well as the open soil. If you have more permanent water-logging in an area of the garden, try growing plants that are suited to these conditions rather than going to the expense of trying to drain the garden.

13. **Wind damage** – as described in other parts of this book, modern housing estate design and impermeable fencing are amongst the greatest causes of wind damage in semi-detached suburbia. Stacking plants with modern 'hoops and other expensive plant support devices does not take away the root cause. Using semi-permeable fencing, shrubs, trees and hedges is the best way of managing the destructive power of the wind.

Control – what a strange term this is, particularly in a garden setting, when all around us are micro and macro biota just waiting for the right moment to feed and breed. I prefer to use the terms 'manage' or 'reduce' as the term control suggests an absolute action whereby the treatment you apply destroys that pest or disease totally. This has not and never will happen in a gardening sense and all we will ever be able to achieve is a reduction in the problem to the point at which we can live with the effects. I have given my thoughts on pest and disease management in no particular order but prefer to see the use of traditional chemical compounds as the absolute last resort, not the first.

Companion planting – if you have never considered this concept as a way of helping to reduce the problems that nature chooses to throw at us, I suggest that you read on as it is more interesting and complex than you might think. It includes some accepted but not always proven ideas on planting two or more different species together for the mutual benefit of each one, the complex world of parasitic plants that have to live together and the strange and sometimes controversial world of allelopathy, where one plant can prevent others from growing near it by exuding biochemicals into the soil. In addition, the very strange world of 'soil-sickness' must be given some thought as it affects some of our most common garden plants. The use of bio-pesticides is part of the companion planting story – one of the latest examples is the use of specific types of mustard plants that exude chemicals into the soil that can kill off eelworms that attack potatoes. It is perhaps one of the many reasons why our forebears, who knew nothing of these complex sciences, carried out crop rotation and avoided monoculture.

Whatever you final opinion of this ancient and complex science, the more you mix your garden plants, herbs, fruit and vegetables up, in a cottage garden style, the less likely you are to have any major problems.

Biological pest control – probably the most natural of all techniques for pest control, this has been developing since the beginning of life on this planet as one organism has evolved to eat another, from the most microscopic forms of life to the largest predators. Over the last century or so, as the human race has evolved to its present state, we have insisted on moving organisms around the globe, with little understanding of how they might manage when they are not in their native, natural environment.

Just to clarify, the word *pest* in this context is any living organism that can cause harm to a plant, including insects, diseases and weeds.

Examples of mistakes from across the globe include the Great Prickly Pear invasion in Australia in the early part of the 20th Century. The *Opuntia monacantha* cactus had been brought into Australia by the British so that they could 'crop' a scale insect called Cochineal (*Dactylopius coccus*) from it for the production of Coccineal, a red dye needed for the red uniforms of the British Army! Although this insect is a natural pest of the cactus, it cannot kill out the plants on its own. Guess what happened! The cactus escaped into the wild and took over vast areas of land. Thankfully *Cactoblastis cactorum*, the Cactus Moth, was discovered as an effective biological control mechanism and gradually the Prickly Pear receded to the point now where it is tolerated and managed.

Since those early disasters, we have developed the biological control industry much further and it now includes a vast range of parasitic organisms, predatory creatures, fungi, viruses, bacteria, naturally occurring products and pheromones that now go under the umbrella of bio-pesticides. These managed populations of bio-pesticides are used widely in the commercial horticultural industry and are progressively being adopted by the home gardener as manufactured pesticides vanish from the shelves of Garden Centres. Only time will tell whether we have made any more blunders, as our human arrogance seems to prevent us from thinking we can do no wrong! Watch this space.

Cultural pest and disease control – this multi-faceted method is one that few gardeners seem to be able grasp properly and yet it forms the basis of all good garden practices that an organic gardener will follow quite naturally:-

1. **Good health** – give a plant the conditions that it requires to perform at its best, including soil conditions, correct seasons, climatic conditions, food and water and it will be able to defend itself from the ravages of pests and diseases far better. This concept is no different in the animal world. The principle of the 'survival of the fittest' is one that nature has created and will continue to use in our gardens and in the wild.

2. **Good plant selection** – start with a healthy young plant or seed and you have the beginnings of a good adult plant – free of pests and diseases and some recognised resistance to associated pathogens at the time of purchase must be the start of a healthy life. Good quality fruit trees, bushes and canes will arrive with a plant health certificate that guarantees them to be free of disease, if not resistant to them. The same is true of seed potatoes from good suppliers. In the human world this might be called eugenics but in the plant world it is about choosing good plants and avoiding the weak and susceptible ones.

3. **Crop rotation** – although, in the average garden or allotment, this concept does not always produce the results that we might expect, it does help to reduce the build up of some soil pests and diseases as well as giving the crops that follow the best soil conditions to survive. Before you start using this idea, you may need to adopt a bed system of vegetable production to make the management of crop rotation a little easier – 4 or 5 year rotations are the norm.

4. **Plant care** – this is the part of gardening that is so essential to ensure the survival of our favourite plants. Examples include:-

    a) the use of clean, sharp pruning tools to prevent excessive damage to plant tissue that then exposes it to the ravages of some fatal viral or fungal attack. See knives and sharpening tools in Chapter 8.

b) carrying out pruning operations using the correct method at the correct time of year so as not to expose the plant, or parts thereof, to the ravages of our climate or some devastating disease.

c) removing dead, diseased and damaged material from plants as soon as they are spotted to avoid secondary infection by unseen fungi, carrying out watering,

d) heating and ventilation of protected crops at the right time of day to avoid the build up of stagnant air that is so loved by certain fungi.

Natural resistance - natural resistance and susceptibility is part of the incredible diversity of the natural world, including the human race and, like the pests and diseases that try to attack, the level and longevity of the resistance or susceptibility varies, keeping us constantly on our toes. Total immunity is rare in the natural world and has only been achieved for the human race to various devastating human diseases such as Small Pox by vaccinations over the last 100 years or so.

Physical pest and disease control – to quote the well known Horticulturist, the late Joe Maiden from here in Yorkshire, squashology is one of the most effective ways of reducing pest and disease problems. Remove the evidence from the plant or soil, dispose of it away from your garden, and you will have some satisfaction that at least some of the living organisms have been removed from the equation. Of course, this requires constant vigilance and good eye sight as well as some advanced knowledge of when and where the pest or disease is likely to occur.

One excellent example used by Joe to help reduce the damage caused by the wireworm involved using an old potato on a piece of wire. The potato is buried underground, with the wire protruding above soil level. Every week or so you lift the potato by pulling on the wire and, if you are lucky, inside you may find one or two wireworm grubs – squashology then becomes the control method of choice.

Nowadays, physical barriers are amongst the most effective. Collars around the base of a newly planted Brassica to stop Cabbage Root Flies or horticultural fleece over a bed of carrots to prevent Carrot Root Flies from laying their eggs are two obvious examples. But they both need a little extra knowledge to ensure that your efforts can be wholly successful. When do the adults first appear? What are the particular habits of the adults? Do they attack other crops that might also need protection?

Other examples worthy of your consideration that fit into this category include: Pheromone traps to catch an unwary male codling moth, hopefully before he finds a female; sticky traps in glasshouses (these may trap beneficial creatures as well and are only really designed to help monitor pest populations) and sticky traps on fruit trees in autumn and winter to catch winter moth females. Used successfully, these methods will help to ensure that the food crops that you harvest and feed to your family are free of all chemicals and that your harvested crops have a little less damage from pests and diseases!

Organic chemical control – as the range of traditional pesticides gradually reduces, particularly in the amateur gardening world, the range of organic and mineral alternatives has increased proportionately. It is now beholding on all of us that are attempting to grow good quality organic plants, to select these from the shelves of the various retail outlets for those occasional 'problems' that seem to plague us and to reject those more traditional pesticides once and for all. Your investment in these organic alternatives will help to fund further development of organic chemicals and will gradually bring the price of these products down – market forces can move mountains. Remember that the commercial growers are now using such products as bio-fumigants to help rid their soils of pest and disease problems – we need to keep up with them and adopt these innovations.

Safe use of pesticides – if, despite your best organic methods of pest and disease control, one or more of these organisms forces you to resort to the use of chemicals, there are a number of well-established rules that you are advised to follow. These will help to ensure that you do not cause any unnecessary harm to anything other than the pest or disease that your efforts are focussing on:

1. *Ask yourself whether you have tried all other avenues before using this as a last resort! Cultural, physical and biological methods are now the preferred options and should be considered before any chemical.*

2. Only use chemicals for which there is current EU and Government approval (www.hse.gov.uk).

3. Read the instructions fully and carefully before you make any attempts at using them and work according to those instructions, without deviation

– doubling the dose does not mean that the product will be twice as effective!

4. Ensure that you have all the necessary personal protective equipment to protect yourself during the application and that any vulnerable adults or children are kept away from the treatment area until it is considered 'safe' for them to return.

5. Ensure that any equipment that you use to apply the chemicals is appropriate and in good working order.

6. Do not apply chemicals during the middle of the day – this helps to ensure that you do not cause any harm to non-pest insects such as bees and hoverflies that are not active early in the morning or later in the evening. Remember that bumble bees can be active at lower temperatures than honey bees. I have seen them active at 5 am on a summer morning and they are still active at 9 pm on a summers evening.

7. Only mix as much chemical as you need for the problem and do not dispose of any surplus diluted chemical into any watercourses, including domestic drains or sewers.

8. Protect sensitive and susceptible crops during application.

9. Any surplus, unwanted concentrated chemicals and containers should be disposed of through an approved authority – check with your Local Authority or on www.hse.gov.uk.

10. **Always store unused chemicals in a frost-free place, away from any direct sunlight and make sure that they are secure to prevent vulnerable children or adults from having access.**

   Tolerance – unlike our forebears, our modern society's attitudes to the problems that are visited on our gardens should be more forgiving. With better communications, more access to knowledge, scientific research, a strong and growing organic movement and, generally, a more environmentally friendly society, you might have thought that our attitude to pests, diseases and weeds would have become a little more tolerant of small amounts of damage and loss. As the range of pesticides that we have available to us gradually declines, surely, we will have to change our ideas and attitudes, wont we! And yet I am still asked what chemical can be used to kill out a temporary invasion of aphids on a rose.

People seem to want to kill anything in their gardens that was not invited in, whether it is a fox searching out a mouse or even an aphid feeding on some 'precious' plant. Most of these creatures have no intention of destroying your garden and are usually only temporary visitors, often only for a few days. With so many environmentally friendly, non-chemical ways of reducing the effects of these 'pests' without destroying their entire population, isn't it time that we changed the way we think?

To quote a variety of people, including Jimi Hendrix, one Dr. William Ellery Channing and Sri Chinmoy Ghose, who seem to have claimed this wonderful statement for themselves:

> **"We look forward to when the 'power of love' will replace the 'love for power.' Then will our world know the blessings of peace."**

This statement is true of every aspect of our society today but particularly in the context of our endless and futile battle with the natural world. Perhaps we should all pin it up on the door of our garden sheds!

Chapter Ten

The Hard Works
of Gardening

Our England is a garden, and such gardens are not made
By singing: "Oh, how beautiful!" and sitting in the shade,
While better men than we go out and start their working lives
At grubbing weeds from gravel paths with broken dinner knives.

Rudyard Kipling (1911)
From: The Glory of the Garden

NO, THIS IS not a chapter dedicated to reducing the physical exertion that is so often associated with gardening, although it is one of the benefits of gardening, but to the solid surfaces that we must all have in our gardens to allow us access to doors, sheds, washing lines, dustbins and all the other necessities of modern living as well as the boundaries that form a line between properties or divide garden areas from one another.

Like all other aspects of our 21st Century lives, hard landscaping has become an art form, with thick catalogues of photographs and extravagant descriptions of all the various types and styles of walls, fences and path surfaces for us to choose from, let alone more websites than you can shake a stick at.

This creates its own problems for us all as we sit staring at the catalogues or aimlessly wander up and down the rows of hard landscaping materials at our local DIY store trying to choose between a vast range of styles of fencing or an unbelievable selection of paving slabs. The simple solution to these dilemmas is to start by looking at the building materials used in the construction of your house or in the local area so that your choice does not create some visual nightmare for you or your neighbours. If you live in a stone house, use stone or stone coloured building materials; if you live in a brick built house, use brick or brick coloured building materials. This complementary selection then allows you a little more leeway when it comes to selecting plants as you may want them to contrast with the house in order to make them stand out or choosing paint and preservative colours for gates, fences, doors etc, thus giving your property an individual touch without ruining the overall image of the street, estate or area. Walk up and down your own streets if you do not believe me but wear a pair of dark glasses whilst you are doing it, firstly to protect your eyes from garish choices and secondly to prevent others from seeing your eyes scanning their houses – the variations on hard landscaping themes that your neighbours use will give you ideas to choose from or ideas to avoid like the plague!

Gravel gardens – this gardening idea is not new and was used widely in the pre and post Second World War periods by garden designers who built alpine gardens, or rockeries as they used to be called. The gravel areas were often at the bottom of a bank of rocks and soil, attempting to simulate the scree slopes that are a natural part of any alpine / mountainous region. The modern interpretation is to have areas of gravel that look like miniature Chesil Beaches or poor copies of Japanese gardens, with a few randomly placed specimen plants and perhaps a few 'ornaments' carefully positioned. These features do little to support wildlife unless planted with the right plants, are often out of place and, if badly constructed or poorly maintained, become a weed infested mess within a relatively short space of time. Deep gravel, up to 150mm deep, avoids weed problems for up to 10 years and well chosen plants will not become a trap for leaves that gradually get ground up by the gravel, making a rich compost for weeds to grow in. Do not plant deciduous trees or shrubs in the gravel as this problem becomes even more exaggerated but select non-invasive, easily managed plants that like a freely drained situation and, if you can, ensure that they provide at least some value to wildlife as a food source – nectar and pollen being the starting point.

Patios – these essential features of the modern garden, whether for sunbathing, barbequing, quiet contemplation or convenient access from house to garden, are almost neutral when it comes to supporting wildlife, although the air gaps under paving slabs that inevitably occur, no matter how expertly they are laid, will provide living quarters for slugs, snails, ants, centipedes and other small creatures – they find their way in and out through gaps in the pointing and many are nocturnal, leaving you with the impression that the patio is a dead zone in the garden. Whether you should constantly chase round filling in the gaps in the pointing is your choice but these gaps can of course become homes for *Taraxicum officinale* (dandelion) and *Poa annua* (annual meadow grass) very quickly. I am not going to discuss the modern wooden decking patios because anyone who has had one constructed will, by the time they read this book, know that they made the wrong decision! Your choice of stone or reconstituted concrete slabs is huge and you should heed my words in the introduction to this chapter before you go out and order a lorry load.

Of course, one of the most critical aspects of laying a patio is to make sure that you get the location and size right for the garden and for the proposed use of said patio. Most gardens have sunny corners and shady ones, sheltered spots and windy ones and so it is as well to analyse the garden environment during the spring and summer months to gauge where these often small microclimates are so that your patio(s) can serve its / their purpose almost as soon as the pointing is dry.

To add an additional benefit for you and any visiting wildlife, why not leave small spaces in the patio so that you can plant a few pavement plants to soften the affect and perhaps even provide you and your family with something edible or colourful (see Appendix 1 for suggestions)

Access paths – the two commonly used materials of gravel and slabs leave little to the imagination but provide the simplest and cheapest solution for most people. Add brick, stone or concrete edging to retain the path and you can have a very acceptable feature in the garden that serves a very useful purpose. Take care when planting close to paths as your access up and down these essential thoroughfares may be hindered by swarms of pollinating insects, some of which do not like being disturbed - one of those strange dilemmas that the true wildlife-friendly gardener has to cope with. The width of the paths should be carefully thought out before any material purchase or excavation works. Do two people need to pass by one another? Is wheelchair access required? Does your choice of building material or surface control the width of a path? Does the path serve some other purpose not previously considered? Can the path be made to serve more than one purpose? Answer these questions and more besides before you start to avoid wasting time and money and to avoid frustration afterwards if you have got things wrong.

Bins and things – every home these days has to have a collection of containers to provide temporary storage of an ever-wider assortment of recyclable materials and the necessary dustbin for general, non-recyclable, non-compostable, non-reusable waste. In this age of trendy garden design and apparently higher standards of living, the dustbin and its relatives are seldom mentioned, let alone given their own distinct garden space. Do the self-appointed upper echelons of our society not generate any waste? Although the compost heap(s) (see Chapter 10 for more ideas and information on composting) may be better placed at the far end of the garden, the routinely used bins should have their own allotted space in the garden, screened, disguised or hidden by all means, but convenient to the family via one house door or another.

Fences and walls – every garden has these in one form or another but do we choose the best materials to build them of and, once they are constructed, use them wisely and to our advantage? Almost certainly not! A simple knowledge of the four points of the compass will inform you that every one of your fences and walls, regardless of who built or erected them and what material(s) they are constructed of, will face one of the 360 degrees of the compass and so, by definition, will have a distinct micro-climate. (see Chapter 3 for more thoughts on this vital subject). Using this knowledge, and the fact that any vertical solid structure will dramatically increase wind speed and turbulence, your choice of building materials, construction techniques and any subsequent planting on them or by them, must be done carefully to avoid disasters and disappointments. As a simple example, which we have all seen at one point in our lives, a solid, wooden panelled fence placed on the windward side of the garden has a much greater chance of being blown over that an open post and rail or hit and miss fence and the wind speed on the leeward side of the fence can flatten unsuspecting herbaceous plants during a summer storm, no matter how many modern support hoops you put in place and the turbulence can dramatically affect the flying ability and behaviour of insects. Semi-permeable fences, with at least one third of the surface area as air space, will allow the wind to filter through and slow down. So, for every 1 square metre of surface area you should be looking to include at least 300 square millimetres of space.

Boundaries – these curses of semi-detached suburbia are a necessary evil that determines the legal ownership of an area of land. In a domestic property environment, where one garden abuts onto another, these boundaries are owned by one party or another and the details of this responsibility are detailed in the deeds of the property. These details are part of the 'searches' that solicitors carry out when you are buying a property along with such issues as Tree Preservation Orders (TPOs), Conservation Area Orders, Public Footpath / Bridle path access across your land, mineral extraction rights, the legal right to have 'livestock' on the property and many more besides. Once you have determined which boundaries you are responsible for, it is then your choice, given any planning restrictions that might be in force at the time, as to the type, style and cost of the boundary that you erect. The sides and rear of the property may abut onto a neighbour's property and your relationship with them may well influence what you can do. The topography of the land can also influence your choice. Given all these potential restrictions, it is important that the boundary gives you the best growing potential for your garden. A solid wall or fence will isolate you from your neighbours, if that is what you want, and can act as a place to grow ornamental or culinarily useful plants but the turbulence created by these impermeable structures may outweigh any of the above advantages. The boundary at the front of the property often has restrictions, particularly in modern estates that tend to be open plan and so high walls and fences are not usually a good idea, unless you want to shut yourself away from the outside world – this is very dependent upon the size and history of the property!

Remember that any solid boundary construction will stop any four-legged wildlife from wandering through your property at night (see Chapter 9 for my image of the badger). Badgers, foxes and hedgehogs travel considerable distances at night in search of a tasty morsel so try to leave at least one part of your boundary open and try to encourage your neighbours to do the same.

To avoid any unnecessary disputes with neighbours, ensure that, before you start work on any boundary projects, you have checked your legal status and have had a 'friendly chat' across the boundary line with your neighbours.

Appendix 1

Plants for a Wildlife Friendly Garden

THIS LIST HAS been compiled over many years of observation in my own garden, in open countryside and in many other gardens across the UK, Ireland and parts of Europe that I have been lucky enough to visit as well as plenty of reading and research in favourite reference books and of course the internet – see Appendices 2, 6 and the Bibliography for more information. It is not an exhaustive or prescriptive list, but allows the reader to pick up ideas on which specific plants or groups of plants can help to support the various levels of wildlife, from tiny insects to our normal butterflies, moths, bats and birds as well as some of the larger consumers and predators that take the top slots in various food chains and webs.

I have chosen to present them in family groups as most plant families have distinct features within their flowers, fruits and seeds that we, as mere humans, are not always able to appreciate. Colour and scent of flowers are only two of many factors that the wild creatures that visit our gardens might take into account when they are flying or walking around our gardens in search of food - whether it is a quick nectar fix that you see Butterflies searching for, to give it the energy for migration or the search for a mate, or a protein laden pollen supply that a hoverfly looks out for to help it lay larger numbers of top quality eggs for the next generation.

Two initiatives that are helping to advise farmers, growers and gardeners on the plants that are good for pollination, let alone all the other benefits of a large and diverse insect population, are the RHS's Plants for Pollinators campaign (see www.rhs.org.uk for details) and the UK Government's DEFRA Pollinator Strategy published in November 2014. Current knowledge suggests that there are around 1,500 different types of pollinating creatures in the UK.

Currently, the Angiosperm Phylogeny Group (APG111), made up of eminent botanists and taxonomists from across the globe, have published charts and reports on the findings of the group over its 20 + years of existence. This work has reclassified much of the work done by Linnaeus and his counterparts 250 years ago and has moved plants from one family group to another as modern methods of research allow us to see further into the genetic history of the plant and animal worlds. Therefore my use of family names is based on the most up-to-date information available. Any errors in family names or plants represented in those families are not intentional. Check any of them out at www.theplantlist.org for the most up-to-date confirmation.

I have avoided listing varietal and cultivar names as I feel that there are many other publications and catalogues that include this level of detail. One comment that I would like to make here, in case I do not mention it elsewhere, is that, over the last 100 years or so of plant breeding, we have had progressively more and more double flowered forms of plants developed to support our apparent desire for anything bright, large and colourful when it is in flower. Some more recent developments, including genetic modification, have further exaggerated this by giving us sterile flowers – both of these factors make the flowers either inaccessible to pollinating insects or worthless and we should do all we can to avoid them in our gardens unless they are in temporary summer displays in containers and baskets – they add nothing but gaudy colour to our gardens and can only serve to divert and confuse the insect pollinators, let alone rob them of essential pollen and nectar!

The Amaryllis Family (*Amaryllidaceae*) – one of the many families that have been restructured in the APG111 work of the last 20 years. Many of its current representatives are amongst our most beautiful, bulbous garden flowers as well as some essential edible ones and, as you might imagine, these stunning flowers are also loved by our pollinating insects. Watch a busy Queen bumble bee climbing in and out of a daffodil flower and you will know what I mean. Genus include: *Agapanthus, Alliums, Amaryllis, Clivia, Galanthus, Leucojum, Narcissus, Nerine* and *Sternbergia*.

The Carrot Family (*Apiaceae*) – the family that contains such plants as Carrots, Celery, Cow Parsley, Coriander, Fennel, Parsley, and Parsnips may not be at the top of your list to have as flowering plants in your garden, but, if by chance they do, watch out for the swarms of pollinating insects and natural predators such as hoverflies, as they land on the flat umbles to enjoy a nectar and pollen rich feast. In addition, some of this family are used by butterflies and moths to lay their eggs on so that the caterpillars can feed – the list includes the rare (in the UK) and beautiful swallowtail butterfly. This vast family also contains herbs such Caraway, Chervil, Cumin, Dill, Lovage and Sweet Cicely. Some ornamental plants to search out include: *Angelica, Astrantia, Eryngium, Bupleurum and Heracleum*. Watch out for the invasive *Aegopodium podagraria (*ground elder) and the rather dangerous *Heracleum mantegazzianum (*Giant hogweed*)!*

The Holly Family (*Aquifoliaceae*) – *Ilex*, one of the few representatives of this exclusive family, contains a British native tree and, giving the right garden circumstances and the right species and cultivars, will reward you with flowers in spring and berries in autumn for many years. One of the strange phenomena of our native hollies is that, for most species and hybrids, each plant is either male or female and so needs insect pollinators to ensure that the pollen is transferred from one plant to another. So, if you are thinking of buying an Ilex to grace your garden, as a single specimen or as part of a hedge, and provide you and your gardens birds with berries to enjoy throughout the winter and a nesting site in spring, check that you have a mix of male and female plants. There are one or two useful self-fertile hybrids to look out for as well. One of the possible 'bonuses' of encouraging birds to eat holly berries is that you are likely to have baby holly trees cropping up in odd places – you can classify these as 'weeds' if you wish but this process is nature in the raw. If you have ever seen the Holly Blue butterfly in your garden in late spring, the chances are that it has completed part of its life cycle on an *Ilex* plant and, if you see one later in the summer it may well have completed part of its life cycle on a *Hedera* plant. See the ivy family below.

The Ivy Family (*Araliaceae*) – with only three commonly planted representatives of this family commonly grown in British gardens, you might wonder why I am bothering to include it in my list. *Hedera* is perhaps the most often seen in all its wonderful variations but *Aralia* and *Fatsia* can also have a place in our gardens, particularly when you watch the numbers of pollinating insects that you can see when they are in flower. The tiny florets that make up the umbels and racemes of the different Genera, make them perfect additions to the wildlife garden, whether large or small. *Hedera* and *Fatsia*, when producing arborescent growth, flower in the autumn, at a time when many other plants have gone to sleep. I have observed house flies, bumble bees, honey bees, wasps and a variety of Butterflies on a bush *Hedera* in my front garden as late as early November, giving them a useful nectar boost before they cast off their mortal toil, hibernate for the winter or migrate to warmer climates. One moth that can use *Hedera* as part of its life-cycle is the spectacular yellow Swallow-tailed moth, although it will feed on other woody plants as well. The hard work of the pollinators rewards the ever-present blackbirds with Ivy berries in spring as they are beginning their nesting season. To have a bush Ivy, you need to root a few cuttings of the arborescent, flowering growth in early summer. See the holly family for reference to the Holly Blue butterfly.

The Asparagus Family (*Asparagaceae*) – a bit of a shock but this family contains some real surprises now that we have the 2009 version of the APG111 system of angiosperm classification available to us all. From the springtime delights of *Scillas* to the summertime flowers of *Eucomis* and *Hostas*, the family produces lots of small floreted spikes that not only give us lots of pleasure but also produces an abundance of pollen and nectar for any lucky insect that happens upon them. Some of its representatives are not guaranteed to be hardy in all parts of Britain but can be treated as half-hardy perennials, moved into temperate protection during the October to May period when our weather can be a little unkind. Genus include: *Agave, Asparagus, Camassia, Chionodoxa, Convallaria, Cordyline, Eucomis, Hosta, Hyacinthus, Liriope, Muscari, Ophiogogon, Ornithogalum, Polygonatum, Pushkinia, Ruscus* and *Scilla.*

The Birch Family (*Betulaceae*) – predominantly a family of the Northern Hemisphere, the *Betulas* and their relatives may not, at a first glance, seem to be a particularly valuable plant to help support wildlife in our gardens, although from an ornamental and architectural point of view, they are one of the best groups of plants. Watch almost any member of the tit family of birds throughout the year on their favourite trees, the *Betula* and *Alnus*, with high insect populations and a plentiful supply of protein and carbohydrate rich seeds for these delightful creatures to feed on. Watch an agile grey squirrel hanging off the branches of a *Corylus*, in their desperate autumnal search for hazel nuts and this valuable member of the family comes into its own, until of course, the squirrel decides to bury his / her stash of nuts in your precious lawn as their secret larder – they may well return again in spring, when their food supplies are a little depleted and dig up your lawn again, in their search for buried treasure! The family attracts a wide range of butterflies and moths, including the Large Emerald that can feed on *Betula, Alnus* and *Corylus* – have all three in your garden and you increase your chances of supporting this beautiful green moth. The Alder Kitten feeds on *Alnus* and *Betula* and both the strange caterpillar and the adult moth are worth searching for. The Mottled Umber moth feeds on a wide range of trees and shrubs but has a liking for *Corylus* and the adult flies and lays her eggs in winter. *Carpinus* is not commonly planted in suburban gardens but does make a good hedge, retaining its dead foliage in winter as *Fagus,*(not a member of this family) does, that can provide welcome shelter for birds on cold winter days. The Nut-tree Tussock moth and the Dotted Border are possible visitors to the *Carpinus.* Two other Genera to look out for in this family are *Ostrya,* the Hop Hornbeam, and *Ostryopsis.* The fine twigs of some of these trees are much sort after by larger birds for nest building.

The Borage Family (*Boraginaceae*) – with some of its members flowering as early as February and all of them bee friendly, every garden should have a number of representatives to cover the seasons. Look out for *Trachystemon orientalis* as one of the earliest but put it in a part of the garden where it cannot escape! This is followed very quickly by the huge range of *Pulmonarias*, the foliage of which may be pretty but the flowers are more essential to bees. The many variations on the word *Symphytum* will help fill shaded and sunny spots with luxuriant foliage and a plentiful supply of flowers for you and the insects to enjoy, from spring to summer – cut these back after one flush of flowers to get another flush in a few weeks time. The old-fashioned cottage garden *Myosotis* should be used in every garden but watch out as self-seeding can cause you a headache! *Echium* is a wonderful summer flowering annual member of the borage family to have. The Crimson Speckled moth feeds on Borago and Myosotis but is only a migrant into the UK from warmer climes in Europe at present. The Scarlet Tiger moth may be seen on *Symphytum* in the south of the UK and the Flame moth caterpillars may be seen feeding on Cynoglossum in the southern half of the UK. Other members of this important family that are worth searching out include *Anchusa, Borago, Brunnera, Cynoglossum, Cerinthe, Heliotropium, Mertensia* and *Omphalodes*.

The Cabbage Family (*Brassicaceae*) – this family provides us with some important food sources, many of which are essential for healthy living in human beings, including broccoli, cabbage, cauliflower and kale as well as vegetable oils through oil seed rape and the condiment mustard. It also provides the natural insect world with a vital source of food, from the simple actinomorphic four petalled nectar and pollen rich flowers for various bees to the juicy leaves of an unwary cabbage for our two cabbage white butterfly caterpillars. As these all grow as biennials, you might consider leaving one or two plants in after harvesting in winter and early spring so that they can flower and give a few beneficial insects some welcome nectar and pollen – you might even get some seed from it to save and grow for the fun of it. In the ornamental garden, we can enjoy *Alyssum, Arabis, Aubretia, Crambe, Erysimum, Hesperis, Iberis, Lunaria, Matthiola* and *Nasturtium* in flower whilst bees and butterflies enjoy their nectar and pollen rich flowers as an energy source in spring and summer. There are a number of wild species that are vital for the support of butterflies, including *Cardamine pratensis*, the Cuckooflower, which is so important in the completion of the life cycle of the Orange Tip Butterfly, a relative of our Cabbage White Butterflies. Other Brassicaceae family feeders include the Green-veined White, the Silver Y moth and the Pearly Underwing moth.

The Honeysuckle Family (*Caprifoliaceae*) – the recognisable scented flowers of many of the typical representative plants are often followed by succulent fruits, much loved by our garden birds. The flowers are of course easily accessible to honey bees and bumble bees but not usually to hoverflies as they are zygomorphic and so do not present an easy landing pad for such insects. There are a number of moth species that are attracted to climbing *Lonicera* species, including the Mottled Umber and the Lilac Beauty, along with the White Admiral butterfly. Some reclassification has been done over recent years through the various genetic studies and previous members of the family that are valuable wildlife-friendly garden plants include *Diervilla* and *Weigela (Diervilleae)* and *Sambucus* and *Viburnum (Apoxaceae)* have been moved to other family groups, in brackets. The three key plants in this family are *Lonicera*, the true honeysuckles, in their various shrubby and climbing forms; *Leycesteria formosa*, the Himalayan Honeysuckle, with its hanging clusters of flowers that are followed by hanging clusters of deep red fruits in autumn and *Symphoricarpos*, the snow berries, that form those masses of impregnable branches that display the typical white and pink fruits in autumn and winter. My favourite for you to search out:- ***Lonicera x purpusii*** – its first flowers open in late

November and new ones are still opening in March. It has a semi-evergreen to deciduous habit and is one of several shrubby honeysuckles that have delightfully scented flowers – the smell reminds me of those wonderful sherbet dabs from my childhood. On a mild winter's day, when a lone Queen bumble bee decides that it can venture out for a quick nectar fix, this shrub can be guaranteed to be there to provide the necessary food. It can reach two metres high but with careful pruning immediately after flowering, it can be kept to manageable proportions, even in a relatively small garden. Combine it with one of the early flowering less vigorous *Clematis alpina* or *C. macropetala* cultivars for an additional display of flowers in spring. After the humble bumble bee has done its duty, this wonderful shrub will provide the local blackbird population with a feast of heart-shaped, rather unpleasant smelling, red honeysuckle fruits in May and June, to add to its wildlife and garden value. I have observed blue and great tits drinking the nectar from the flowers in winter – a bonus for us and them! Other Genera to search in this family that can give valuable food to wildlife and horticultural satisfaction to us include: *Abelia, Centranthus, Cephalaria, Dipsacus, Kolkwitzia, Knautia, Scabiosa* and *Valeriana.*

Since the initial writing of this appendix **Dipsacaceae**, traditionally known as the Teasel family, has been absorbed into *Caprifoliaceae* but I have included my original text for you to enjoy!

With only four obvious representatives for us to choose from in Britain in this old family, you may think of it as being of little value to us for either ornamental or wildlife purposes. How wrong you would be! One of my absolute favourites is *Cephalaria,* the Giant or Yellow Scabious that flowers in June on 2 metre high stems, with typical flat Scabious flower heads, made up of scores of tiny florets, each with its own larder of pollen and nectar to attract passing bees and hoverflies. Planted near your fruit garden, this will certainly help to increase the crop. The original family representative was of course *Dipsacus fullonum* that flowers in July and August on tall stems, with these flowers being followed by those distinctive seed heads that are so loved by birds such as the Goldfinch. *Knautia macedonica* is a sprawling herbaceous plant that, with a little dead heading, will flower from late June until September, giving a continuous supply of pollen and nectar as well as providing the gardener with a wonderful display of small purple-red Scabious flowers. *Scabiosa,* the pincushion flower, has around 80 wild species and numerous cultivars for us to select from, with tiny alpine forms and tall, graceful herbaceous perennials as well as one or two strange hardy annual forms for us to play with. With the same design of flower as the rest of the family, these long flowering herbaceous plants should grace every garden, whether in their ornamental forms or their native forms so reminiscent of wildflower meadows and roadside embankments. Look out for the Narrow-bordered Bee Hawk-moth if you have a lot of representatives of this family in your garden.

The Daisy Family (*Compositae*) – of all the plant families, the daisy family must produce the most valuable flowers and seeds for the two, four and six legged creatures of our temperate climate. The list of representative plants that I would consider to be vital to a well-managed wildlife friendly garden must include *Bellis perennis* and *Taraxacum officinale* in the lawn, perennial *Aster* species for autumn flowering, annual *Calendulas* for hoverflies and bees, *Doronicums* for an early supply of pollen and nectar for hoverflies and bees, *Echinops ritro* for bees and butterflies in summer, *Achilleas* for hoverflies, *Helianthus* for bees and goldfinches, *Echinacea* and *Rudbeckias* for bees, hoverflies and butterflies. I can hear you asking why as you read through this list – simple, single, flat headed, actinomorphic, open flowers are easy landing pads for all flying creatures and when the flowers are made up of hundreds of tiny florets, you can imagine that it must be like landing at a five star Michelin restaurant – pollen and nectar in a constant supply from March, when the first *Bellis* and

Doronicums open, until November, when the last Asters (Michaelmas daisies) finish. In addition, look out for *Ageratum, Anaphalis, Antennaria, Argyranthemum, Artemesia, Bidens, Brachyglottis, Catananche, Centaurea, Chrysanthemum, Circium, Coreopsis, Cosmos, Crepis, Dahlia, Echinops, Eupatorium, Erigeron, Felicia, Gaillardia, Gazania, Helenium, Inula, Leontopodium, Liatris, Ligularia, Onopordum, Santolina, Senecio, Solidago, Tagetes* and *Tanecetum.* The hoverflies will repay your generosity by helping to keep aphid populations under control throughout the spring and summer months. The list of butterflies and moths that use *Compositae* plants to complete their life-cycles is lengthy but, suffice it to say that the Cinnabar moth, the Large Yellow Underwing moth and the Painted Lady butterfly are amongst them. There are ten different moths capable of feeding on *Taraxacum* alone!

The Spurge Family (*Euphorbiaceae*) – milky sap and Poinsettias are the indicators of this family and it is really only the true *Euphorbias* that we need to concern ourselves with here as most of the spurge family grow in tropical and sub-tropical regions of the world. We have one or two weed plants that are *Euphorbias* that can be nuisance in cultivated ground and, with the milky sap being a potentially severe skin irritant to humans, this group of plants is worth getting to know, if only for personal and family safety. As ornamental plants they can be spectacular, architectural specimens in spring and summer borders. Once the strange flowers appear, the nectar source becomes a major attraction for any insect capable of probing their flowers. I have Euphorbia mellifera in my front garden and it's flowers smell like an open pot of honey – all the bees adore it in April and May. There is also a Spurge Hawk-moth that may find its way into your garden, but only if you live in southern England. One of the strange plants in this Genus is *Euphorbia lathyris*, the mole plant or Caper Spurge, said to deter moles in your garden!

The Beech Family (*Fagaceae*) – although not a large plant family in the scale of things, this family has three very important Genera that provide some of the most valuable trees in Europe. *Castanea* not only provides food for us in the form of Sweet Chestnuts but produces one of the best building timbers. In the South of England it is a woodland tree producing those delicious chestnuts for the Christmas celebrations. *Fagus* is also an important tree for timber but fits into our garden environment as a wonderful hedge, even in smaller gardens, and as a specimen tree in parks, country estates and larger gardens as well as a woodland tree in some parts of the UK. *Quercus* comes in many different guises but is most famous, in environmental terms, for supporting upwards of 200 creatures from minute insects to large owls. It forms some of the most important woodland in this country and, if you are fortunate enough to live on the edge of oak woodland, the wildlife that will visit your garden is likely to greatly increase. So, if your garden is large enough to have a mature or semi-mature *Quercus* in it, I would suggest that you plant one today for future generations of insects, owls and many more besides. The list of butterflies and moths that need these trees to complete their life-cycles is extensive and includes the Purple Hairstreak, the Gypsy Moth and the Copper Underwing. Of course, some of this lengthy list are not friendly to our cultivated plants but that is the balance of nature!

The Cranesbill Family (*Geraniaceae*) – although we are limited, for the most part, in our British climate to three representatives from this family, their value, both ecologically and aesthetically, should not be downgraded. The true *Geranium* that we grow in our herbaceous borders is amongst the most popular source of pollen and nectar for bumblebees in summer, with its easily accessible flowers and relatively long flowering season, particularly if you grow a range of different species and hybrids and the Brown Argus butterfly can use some of them as a food source for their caterpillars. Some Geraniums come into flower as early as April and, if you cut back early flowering types, some will produce a second flush in late summer, giving both you and the bees an extended season of pleasure. For those that have alpine gardens, well-drained gravel gardens or suitable alpine containers, the *Erodiums* (Storksbills) deserve a place, again with their invitingly simple flowers in great numbers and their ease of care, they make an excellent addition to the selection of plants from this family that you and your wildlife can enjoy. Perhaps the most popular Genus is the *Pelargoniums* that are so often incorrectly called Geraniums. With a wide range of cultivars and colours to choose from and types suited to hanging baskets as well as borders, this Genus gives summer pleasure to us as well as any visiting insects looking for a quick pollen or nectar fix.

The Iris Family (Iridaceae) - like many of the monocotyledonous families, Iridaceae has been restructured, with Genus being moved to suit the new APG111 understanding and knowledge. With many plants growing from corms and rhizomes and originating from the Southern Hemisphere, the cultivation and care of these often spectacular garden plants can cause some gardeners problems. For our resident insect populations there are no such problems as the zygomorphic flowers are often large and easily accessible even for the clumsiest of insects. Plants include: *Crocosmia, Crocus, Dierama, Fressia, Gladiolus, Iris, Ixia, Sparaxis, Tigridia, Tritonia* and *Watsonia.*

The Dead Nettle Family (Labiatae / Lamiaceae) – the dead nettle family includes some very good culinary, medicinal and ornamental plants for us such as *Ajuga, Calamintha, Hyssopus, Lavendula, Melissa, Mentha, Monarda, Nepeta, Origanum, Perovskia, Phlomis, Prunella, Rosmarinus, Salvia, Stachys* and *Thymus* but is also contains such valuable insect pollinator plants as *Lamium,* that can support bees from as early as January in a mild winter. Butterflies and moths use the flowers of many of these plants as a quick and easy nectar source because they consist of lots of tiny flowers that are easy to land on and have short flower tubes that allow easy access to the pollen and nectar. One of the delights of wildlife gardening is that you have more time to observe the goings on in the garden and, during the warm summer of 2014 I saw the Mint Moth for the first time – this tiny little maroon coloured daytime flying moth uses *Mentha, Thymus* and *Origanum* to lay its eggs. This was repeated in the hot summer of 2018 when the Mint moth visited again. Because of the aromatic nature of most of these plants, they are often used in companion planting to help deter and confuse detrimental insects. One of the many strange anomalies of the natural world!

The Pea Family (Leguminosae / Fabaceae) – the third largest of all plant families, with more than 700 Genera and over 20,000 species. It contains some of the world's most important food crops, let alone some of our best garden plants. Although the Genera includes plants that we may classify as weeds, such as black medick, clover and vetch, it also contains some of the world's most important food crops such as peas and beans and a vast list of wild plants and cultivated plants for both wildlife and us to enjoy. I have listed a small representation of the Genera that we can grow in our gardens as trees, shrubs, climbers and herbaceous plants to give you a flavour: *Baptisia, Cercis, Colutea, Coronilla, Cytisus, Genista, Gleditsia, Laburnum, Lathyrus, Lotus, Lupinus, Medicago, Phaseolus, Piptanthus, Pisum, Sophora, Spartium, Trifolium, Ulex, Vicia* and *Wisteria.* Many of these plants attract butterflies and moths such as the Green Hairstreak, Common Blue and the Six-spot Burnet. Bees are attracted to some of these plants but the zygomorphic flowers are not suited to hoverflies as the design of the flowers does not suit their flying habits. One of the other benefits of having members of this family in your garden is that they can provide a free source of nitrogen. With the help of nitrogen fixing bacteria that extract nitrogen from the atmosphere and fix it on the roots of Leguminous plants, we can take advantage of this symbiotic relationship in our garden practices – crop rotation of leguminous crops followed by leafy crops that can use the nitrogen.

The Poppy Family (Papaveraceae) – watch any pollinating insect, from an agile hoverfly to a clumsy queen bumble-bee in an open poppy flower, and their desperation for the plentiful and rich pollen and nectar is very obvious. The representative Genus's of this family will provide this abundant supply from mid spring through to late summer, mostly with brightly coloured flowers, if you grow a good range: *Corydalis, Dicentra, Eschscholzia, Fumaria, Glaucium, Macleaya, Meconopsis, Papaver, Romneya* and *Sanguinaria* will show you the links between the different Genus's. Some of the annual and biennial species may become a nuisance in the garden because of their ability to produce vast quantities of seed, often distributed by the action of the wind as it shakes the seed pods back and forth but they are easy to remove selectively so that you maintain a stock of plants for flowering.

The Plantain Family (Plantaginaceae) – *Antirrhinum, Asarina, Bacopa, Chelone, Digitalis, Erinus, Hebe, Linaria, Parahebe, Penstemon, Plantago* and *Veronica* are amongst the representative Genus's in this re-organised plant family and you can see that there are some important garden plants amongst them for us as well as the two, four, six and eight legged creatures that may choose our gardens as their temporary or permanent homes. Watch a worker bumble-bee fighting its way into the tube of a Digitalis flower and you will know that the family is able to provide vital food for these essential insects. Watch a family of Greenfinches or Goldfinches feeding on the seed heads of any member of the *Plantago* Genus and you will immediately welcome those strange wildflowers into your garden, if not into your lawn! The thousands of tiny florets produced by any member of the Genus *Hebe* allow a wide variety of insects to feed from the nectaries as a source of energy.

The Grass Family (Poaceae / Graminae) – as wind is the only pollinator for this family, you might wonder why I have included it in this Appendix. Check out the number of butterfly and moth species that rely heavily on the grasses as food plants in their caterpillar stages and the number of bird species that rely on grass seeds for food or dead grass for nesting material and you will begin to see that grasses, in all their strange and diverse guises, are an essential group of plants to have in our gardens, let alone the wider countryside. A recent and delightful example that chose to visit our garden was a Gatekeeper butterfly that completes its lifecycle on a variety of grass species. Of course, I am not referring to the mown features that we choose to call lawns because, for the most part, these are sterile environments. Neither am I directly referring to the vast numbers of Poaceae representatives that provide us with much of our staple food. The family is the fifth largest in the hierarchy of the plant world, with over 10,000 species and more than 600 Genera and covers more than 20% of the world's land surface in what is broadly described as grassland. In our own gardens, grasses are seen as a weekly chore to cut, a few weeds that rear their heads in our beds and borders or, more so in recent years, as an ornamental plant that gives us pleasure. Amongst the Genera for us to consider, the following are just a small representation of those thousands of variations that we can enjoy or curse in our gardens: *Acrostis, Arundinaria, Briza, Calamagrostis, Cortaderia, Deschampsia, Elymus, Fargesia, Festuca, Hakonechloa, Holcus, Hordeum, Imperata, Lolium, Milium, Miscanthus, Molinia, Pennisetum, Phleum, Phragmites, Poa, Sasa, Stipa* and *Zea*.

The Dock Family (Polygonaceae) – some might call this the dock family and, yes, it does contain docks as well as a number of other problem weeds such as *Fallopia japonica, Polygonum aviculare* and several other *Rumex* species, including sorrels, some of which are edible. However, because of the large numbers of tiny flowers on each flower spike, the amount of nectar and pollen available to visiting insects is incredible. For some species, this is followed by large numbers of seeds that are tasty morsels for seed-eating birds such as the finches. Within the family, one of the more ornamental plants are the *Persicarias* – this delightful collection of herbaceous perennials, previously named *Polygonum,* all have long panicles of small funnel shaped flowers that are loved by many insects but particularly honey bees and wasps. Plant early flowering species such as *Persicaria bistorta* near soft fruit bushes to help encourage bees to pollinate the flowers. Later flowering species such as *P. amplexicaule* are very attractive in flower but are also loved by late flying butterflies and bees, particularly if grown in full sun. Of course, if you have the invasive *Fallopia japonica* in your garden, it may support insects when in flower but it will drown everything else out in its path.

The Primula Family (Primulaceae) – one of the most beautiful of all flowers for our gardens, with a few surprises contained within it to extend the flowering season for us and any wild garden visitors. For the most part, the flowers are open and so allow access to pollinating insects, giving the plants the chance to spread seed and maintain their position in the garden or wild environment. *Anagallis, Androsace, Cyclamen, Dodecatheon, Lysimachia, Primula* and *Soldanella* will provide you with flowers across the seasons, from early spring to late autumn in a variety of garden environments.

The Rose Family (Roseacea) – probably one of the most important families for wildlife, let alone us. The flowers provide incredible opportunities for pollinating insects across autumn, winter, spring and early summer, but the results of their labours are perhaps even more important – the fruits that the animal world and humans can harvest from the spring and early summer efforts of bees and other pollinating provides unmeasureable tonnages of succulent, flavoursome, nutritious food for us all to enjoy. Here I have listed just a selection but don't let it limit you in your search for others: *Amelanchier, Aronia, Chaenomeles, Cotoneaster, Crataegus, Cydonia, Fragaria, Malus, Mespilus, Prunus, Pyracantha, Pyrus, Rosa, Rubus* and *Sorbus.* In addition to these fruiting plants, you might also search out one or two surprising shrubby and herbaceous members of this family that, although not producing succulent fruits for consumption, do provide pollen and nectar sources for a wide variety of insects, let alone ornamental pleasure for us, namely: *Acaena, Alchemilla, Aruncus, Dryas, Exochorda, Filipendula, Geum, Kerria, Physocarpus, Potentilla, Sanguisorba* and *Spiraea.*

The Buttercup or Crowfoot Family (Ranunculaceae) – the ubiquitous buttercup family, with more than 60 Genera and 1,500 species worldwide. Whether it is the rampaging *Clematis vitalba* in a southern wood or the creeping *Ranunculus repens* in a damp northern lawn, this family is within sight of almost every human being in Britain. The large majority of the members of this family have large numbers of bright, open flowers or hundreds of tiny florets, making them particularly attractive to pollinating insects. Some species are essential food plants for moths such as the Marsh Carpet Moth and the Beaded Chestnut Moth. Plants to search out include: *Aconitum, Actaea, Adonis, Anemone, Aquilegia, Caltha, Cimicifuga, Clematis, Delphinium, Eranthis, Helleborus, Nigella, Pulsatilla, Ranunculus* and *Thalictrum.* These span the seasons from early spring to late autumn, giving hungry wildlife plenty of opportunity to feed and also to give you pleasure.

The Maple Family (Sapindaceae syn. Acereae) – stare up at the crown of a mature *Acer campestre* in April and you will not only see the pale yellow clusters of tiny flowers but the buzz of honey bees and worker bumble bees desperately gathering supplies of pollen and nectar to take back to their hives to help feed the new broods of larvae. So when you plant up your wildlife friendly garden, don't forget to include one or two Acers to add some vital pollen and nectar to the larder for our insects. Of course, you might already be aware that a number of aphid species find Acers very tempting in the spring and early summer – these tiny creatures might be a nuisance to us but to a wide variety of insects including parasitic wasps, ants, hoverflies and our normal wasps, they are a source of food – just do not park your car under a large mature specimen as it will be covered in the excreted sticky waste of aphids known as honeydew, which is followed usually by the Sooty Mould fungus that grows on the sugar, turning everything black as well as sticky. Other Genera in this renamed family include *Aesculus* (Horse chestnuts) and *Koelreuteria* (Golden Rain tree or Pride of India), both of which can support pollinating insects when in flower in late spring or early summer.

The Figwort Family (Scrophulariaceae) – the family name was one of the first that I learnt as a young sixteen year old apprentice, because it had a nice sound to it and it rolled off the tongue easily. The family contains some old garden favourites as well as one or two wild flowers if you choose to allow them across your garden boundary. The multi-floreted flower heads not only provide us with excellent floral displays in summer but also offer very good feeding opportunities for any insect that chooses to alight on them. We are probably all very familiar with the benefits of having *Buddleias* in the garden that give so much support to the migratory and resident butterfly and moth populations but there are a number of other rewards that we might get if we grow this range of plants. *Verbascum* attracts the Mullein moth with its dramatically contrasting colours as a caterpillar. *Scrophularia*, the Common Figwort, supports the Water Betony, a close relative of the Mullein moth, although it is not common in the UK apart from in the south. One relatively recent introduced pest is the tiny, black and white Figwort weevil that can ruin the flowering potential of *Phygelius* and *Scrophularia*. Look out for any of the following - *Buddleia, Calceolaria, Diascia, Nemesia, Phygelius, Scrophularia, Verbascum.*

The Tomato Family (Solanaceae) - as one of the most important families for providing food for our ever increasing population, the tomato family contains some obvious examples and a few surprises. The first is that almost exclusively, the family originates from South America, with many of its representatives being moved around the world following the Spanish invasion in the late 15th century headed by Christopher Columbus. We now enjoy many of the *Solanum* species, including Potatoes, Tomatoes and Aubergines as well as *Physalis* and *Capsicum* as edible plants in our gardens and at the local supermarket. However, in our own gardens, whether we grow these outdoors or under some form of protection, they all need insect pollinators to help produce the fruits that we have come to enjoy. Of course, potatoes (*Solanum tuberosum*) do not require any pollinators to give us one of our most important stable foods as we harvest an underground stem tuber. If the flowers that we see at harvest time do get pollinated, the plant may develop the very poisonous potato fruits – you have been warned! In addition to these edible crops, the family contains some excellent ornamental plants that are much loved by a variety of insects – these include: *Brugmansia, Datura, Nicandra, Nicotiana, Petunia* and *Schizanthus*. One plant that you not want to encourage in your garden, although it may jump the wrong way over the garden wall, is *Atropa belladonna*, the Deadly Nightshade as it has the potential to cause serious harm if fruits are ingested. It still requires insects to pollinate it and commercially, the drug Atropine is derived from the plant so it is not necessarily as negative as we might think.

MORE IDEAS ON PLANTS FOR WILDLIFE IN THE GARDEN

Mixed hedges – highlighted in Chapter Two, the more diverse a hedge is the greater the number of animal and insect species will use it for shelter, breeding and feeding, helping to establish and maintain a healthy balance of positive and negative wildlife. Use the following species to make an excellent mixed, double row hedge that only needs cutting once a year in late summer! *Acer campestre, Cotoneaster simonsii. Crataegus monogyna* or *C. oxycantha, Fagus sylvatica, Ilex aquifolium, Rosa canina.* If one of the species does not give a top performance in one year, you can be assured that another species will do well in place of it. Its mix of evergreen and deciduous trees / shrubs helps to make it a perfect shelter site during inclement weather as well as an excellent nesting site for some garden birds and, if you feel that you need it, you will get privacy.

Trees - used as escape routes for small birds from garden predators, feeding sites for thousands of insects, roosting and nesting sites for birds, ornamental features for us humans and one of the best ways of storing all that surplus carbon that we keep on producing, let alone providing aerobic creatures with oxygen, trees are an essential element of every garden, almost no matter what the size. They can also be productive if you choose the right species, from the flowers for the pollinating insects to the seeds, fruits and nuts for us and the wildlife that so enjoy eating them. It is almost impossible to list all the trees that can give us true horticultural and environmental benefits but the various species and hybrids of *Acer, Aesculus, Alnus, Amelanchier, Betula, Cotoneasters, Cydonia, Fagus, Malus, Mespilus, Prunus, Pyrus, Quercus, Sorbus,* and *Tilia* are just a few commonly available Genera that immediately come to mind.

Pavement and Patio plants – to help soften the visual impact of paved areas and to absorb some of the heat that is radiated from them, let alone providing us with ornamental and culinary plants to enjoy, there are a vast range of plants that can be grown in between paving slabs. Herbs such as *Lavendula, Salvia officinalis, Rosmarinus* and *Thymus* are perhaps the first to come to mind, preferring the hot, dry, sunny environment of paved areas as they do. The high light and high temperatures help to concentrate the essential oils in these Mediterranean type plants, making the scents and flavours more intense. Note that there is little point in using these examples if your paths and patios do not receive at least half of the summer daylight hours. Other more ornamental alpine plants to look out for include: *Acaena spp, Alchemilla spp, Antennaria dioica, Armeria spp, Dianthus spp, Erodium spp, Geranium spp, Iberis sempervirens, Mentha requienii, Phlox spp, Saponaria spp, Sedum spp* and *Sempervivum ssp.* For more ideas on this quite specific group of plants visit one or two alpine nurseries or search through the alpine section of your local garden centre. Take care to choose plants that do not have an invasive roots, rhizomes, stolons or tubers - you may regret the choice after a few years as your path or patio becomes infested with them. Remember that most of the plants for these situations are excellent for attracting pollinating and other beneficial insects such as hoverflies, butterflies and moths and few if any suffer from any major pest or disease problems, reducing your need to consider the use of pesticides.

Native wildflowers – although the large majority of our garden plants do not originate from the British Isles, most gardeners do not seem to be particularly concerned! Historically, as the various invaders and plant hunters, from the Roman times onwards, brought plants to our shores from every corner of the globe, we became accustomed to seeing and using these plants for culinary, medicinal and aesthetic purposes. It is true to say that we probably could not survive today without many of them but, unfortunately, the native flora that are associated with various native fauna, have slowly had to give way to these foreign invaders. So, by recognising and then growing a number of local or regional wildflowers in our gardens, under our care, we might be helping to redress the balance in the natural environment and, at the same time, provide somewhere for native fauna to feed and survive. It must be remembered that wild flowers do not want to be grown in a rich, organic soil with copious amounts of water and fertilizer; in fact they require the complete opposite, making the amount of care that we have to give much less.

Coastal gardens – if you live within smelling distance of the sea, you are likely to need suitable plants for that very specific environment, either to cope with the salt spray or to protect normal garden plants from it. If the species name of the plant is '*maritima*' or '*littoralis*' it will almost certainly cope. One way of ensuring that your coastal garden can survive is to study the local native coastal flora and to study the flora of other gardens in the locality to see what can survive this often harsh and unforgiving environment. By using local and regional plants that can cope with your version of coastal climate, you are more likely to support local and regional insects and other creatures. Some of the advantages to living in a coastal environment are that there are less damaging frosts due to the warming influence of the sea and better light levels due to the reflective qualities of the sea, both of which give the gardener the opportunity to grow more tender species in summer and to benefit from a longer flowering season for many plants.

Hardy annual borders and annual wildflower borders – the latest terminology for us all to get our heads around is 'shake it and rake it.' Whether you are sowing a small drift of one hardy annual or a whole area of mixed annual wild flowers, shaking up the seed packet(s) across the soil and raking the ground after sowing is about all you need to do to guarantee a spectacular display from late June to late September. Unless your soil is, by any measurement, extreme, these easy to grow, resilient annuals will perform well for you in the first summer, only requiring topping up with extra seed each year to add variety to the display. You can save your own seed from your favourites as the seed heads form in August and September, storing the seeds in paper bags overwinter ready for early April and a warm spring day. Some species will willingly seed themselves, with some germinating before the end of summer – in milder winters and sheltered corners these seedlings will get through the winter and will then flower in May and June, giving you and any associated wildlife an extended season of pleasure and opportunity. Seeds to search for at Garden Centres and in seed catalogues include:- *Adonis aestivalis* (Pheasant's Eye), *Agrostemma githago* (Corn Cockle), *Ammi majus* (Bishop's Flower), *Anthemis arvensis* (Corn Chamomile*), Asperula orientalis (*Woodruff*), Briza maxima* (Quaking Grass), *Bromis rubens* (Red Brome*), Calendula officinalis* (Pot Marigold*), Centaurea cyanus* (Cornflower), *Cerinthe major purpurescens* (Honeywort), *Chenopodium giganteum (Tree Spinach*), Clarkia elegans, Collomia biflora, Consolida regalis, Convolvulus tricolor, Cosmos bipinnatus* (Cosmea), *Crepis rubra, Dracocephalum moldavica, Echium vulgare* (Viper's Bugloss), *Eschscholtzia californica*

(Californian Poppy), *Gaillardia aristata, Gilia tricolor* (Blue Eyes), *Godetia grandiflora, Helenium amarum, Helianthus annus* (Sunflower*), Iberis umbellata* (Annual Candytuft*), Jasione Montana* (Sheep's bit), *Lagurus ovatus (*Hare's Tail Grass), *Lavatera trimestris* (Annual Mallow), *Limnanthes douglasii* (Poached Egg Plant), *Linaria maroccana* (Toadflax), *Linum usitatissimum* (Common flax), *Lupinus luteus* (Yellow Lupin), *Malcolmia maritima* (Virginian Stock), *Matthiola bicornis* (Night-scented Stock), *Nemophila menziesii (*Baby blue eyes), *Nicandra physaloides* (Shoo-fly plant), *Nigella damascena* (Love-in-the-Mist), *Omphalodes linifolia* (Venus's Navelwort), *Panicum violaceum, Papaver spps, Phacelia tanacetifolia, Reseda odorata (Mignonette), Saponaria vaccaria* (Soapwort), *Scabiousa atropurpurea* (Annual Scabious), *Setaria italic* (Millet), *Tolpis barbata, Tropaeolum majus* (Nasturtium), *Xerathemum annum.*

Many of these produce good cut flowers and dry flowers for the house as well as attracting and supporting a wide variety of wildlife.

Appendix 2

Websites
Worth Visiting

THIS IS A short but ever-growing list of websites that I feel have some value for the organic or wildlife gardener but of course the addresses and the contents very quickly become obsolete so take care when visiting them and taking information from them. They are in alphabetical order to avoid any indication of priority or personal preference. They are all active at the time of publishing.

Amphibian and Reptile Conservation Trust – www.arc-trust.org – all about our British native amphibians and reptile.

Ants – www.antnest.co.uk – a website for anyone searching for information on ants – well worth a read.

Badger Trust – www.badger.org.uk – a federation of local and regional badger groups across the UK that are helping to protect our native badger population. Help and advice for all.

Bat Conservation Trust – www.bats.org.uk – the clue is in the title. All things bat related in the UK.

Blooms for Bees – www.bloomsforbees.co.uk – a delightful website designed to help promote and improve gardens and gardening for bumblebees in the UK.

British Arachnological Society – www.britishspiders.org.uk – all you ever wanted to know about spiders and a lot more besides.

British Beekeepers Association – www.bbka.org.uk – the British Beekeepers Association website from which you can source regional and local associations for support and advice on beekeeping. You may also like to check out the Bumblebee Conservation Trust at www.bumblebeeconservationtrust.org - the clue to their valuable work is in their title. There are many local and regional groups in Yorkshire that you can join that will help you in those early stages of becoming a beekeeper.

British Bryological Society – www.britishbryologicalsociety.org.uk – for all of you that find mosses and liverworts interesting, this website and the organisation is for you.

British Ecological Society – www.britishecologicalsociety.org – their vision – a world inspired, informed and influenced by ecology. A very worthy organisation with a fantastic website and resources.

British Geological Survey – www.bgs.ac.uk – for all things geological, the BGS has been active since 1835 an, with modern technology is taking our understanding of all things geological to greater heights, or should that be depths?

British Hedgehog Preservation Society – www.britishhedgehogs.org.uk – advise and help to protect our declining hedgehog populations.

British Mammal Society – www.mammal.org.uk – formed in 1954, this society surveys, researches, monitors and helps to conserve the many and varied mammals that choose to call the UK their home. The website allows you access to an app for smart phones so that you can record your observations.

British Mycological Society – www.britmycolsoc.org.uk – this society was set up to promote research, educate and conserve all things fungal. Take a look at www.fungionline.org.uk as well.

British Society for Plant Pathology – www.bcpp.org.uk – set up in 1981, this organisation's main concern is the study of plant diseases. The website has lists of the latest diseases affecting plants across the globe. Not for the faint-hearted but a worthy website nevertheless.

Brogdale Fruit Collection – www.brogdale.org - this incredible collection of over 4,000 cultivars of apples, pears, plums, cherries, bush fruits, vines and cob nuts, based at Brogdale, Faversham, Kent, is jointly managed by the University of Reading, Brogdale Collections (www.brogdalecollections.co.uk), DEFRA (www.defra.gov.uk) and the National Fruit Collection (www.nationalfruitcollection.org.uk) giving both commercial and amateur growers access to identification services, events, advice, plants and propagation material, and much, much more.

Butterflies – www.ukbutterflies.co.uk – in association with www.butterfly-conservation.org. These two websites will provide you with all the information you need to help support the British and migratory butterflies and will help in the identification of species that choose to visit your garden.

Centre for Alternative Technology – www.cat.org.uk – a well-established organisation, based in central Wales that researches environmentally friendly ideas for the home, farm, garden, allotment etc. Some very good publications worthy of consideration and some excellent courses, both academic and practical.

Chilterns Seeds – www.chilternseeds.co.uk – although I would not normally recommend a commercial company in this context, this company, started in 1975 in the dining room of the owners in their house in Oxfordshire, is one of the best for unusual plants and fascinating facts about them. So, even if you never buy any seeds, order the catalogue and enjoy a good read.

The Community Land Advisory Service (CLAS) - www.communitylandadvice.org.uk – a project run by the Federation of City Farms and Community Gardens to provide support and advice to groups setting and running these types of activities across the UK.

Earthworm Society of Britain – www.earthwormsoc.org.uk – the website of the ESB. Allows you to see more of the fascinating world of worms, in all their strange guises.

Eat Weeds – a guide to edible wild plants in Britain – www.eatweeds.co.uk – a fascinating website to help those that want to comb the highways and byways for wild plants that are edible.

England's Community Forests – www.communityforests.org.uk – started in 1990 by the then Countryside Commission. It now has over 10,000 hectares of new woodland in and around urban areas and manages 27,000 hectares of existing woodland. It is also now, alongside the Woodland Trust, beginning work on the new Northern Forest that will run from Liverpool to Hull.

The Royal Entomological Society – www.royentsoc.co.uk – with Her Majesty the Queen as its Patron and over 150 years of history, this society must surely be the ultimate authority on all things insectivorous. The website has a very handy booklet on garden entomology to download free of charge and an excellent collection of fact files on a wide range of insects.

Environment Agency – www.environment-agency.gov.uk – the official website of this government agency. Excellent advisory website. Good leaflets on invasive aquatic weeds.

Federation of City Farms and Community Gardens – www.farmgarden.org.uk – a registered charity acting as an umbrella organisation for any groups and individuals involved in these types of activities.

Field Studies Council – www.field-studies-council.org - established in 1943, the FSC is a leading environmental education charity, providing courses, publications and support for anyone wanting to help encourage us to know and understand the natural world. Its educational charts are used widely in schools, colleges and universities as a point of reference for teachers and students alike.

Findhorn Foundation – www.findhorn.org – a spiritual community, eco-village and international centre for holistic education. Visit the website to fully understand the whole picture of this incredible community. Growing much of their own food is but a small part of what this community does. It has recently celebrated its 50th anniversary.

Food and Environment Research Agency – www.fera.co.uk – this organisation, previously owned and run by Government, provides support and advice to farmers, growers, the food processing industry and many more on food safety, crop health, the environment in which food is produced and much, much more. FERA issues warnings to growers on new pest and disease problems through its news bulletin.

Fresh Water Habitats Trust – www.freshwaterhabitats.org.uk a charitable organisation that focuses its efforts on the protection and development of fresh water habitats for the benefit of wildlife as well as using its vast knowledge base to help educate, influence and inform.

Garden Arena – www.gardenarena.co.uk – a superb up-to-date website with listing of shows, gardens, arboreta, organisations and much, much more.

Garden Museum – www.gardenmuseum.org.uk – started in 1977 as part of a project to preserve the grave of the famous gardener and plant hunter John Tradescant (1570–1638), this museum traces the history of gardens, gardeners and gardening. Make it one of your must do visits the next time you visit London.

Garden Organic – www.gardenorganic.org.uk – originally called the Henry Doubleday Research Association, Garden Organic researches, trials and educates about all matters related to organic gardening. Its Heritage Seed Library is a vital genetic resource for all growers, both commercial and amateur, with many older vegetable cultivars holding essential genetic details of hardiness, disease resistance and flavour that many modern cultivars seem to have lost. Contains some good information on mycorrhiza. The organisation runs courses on a wide variety of organic gardening related subjects.

Global Horticulture Initiative – www.globalhort.org – at long last a way of singing the praises of horticulture globally. Its four core activities are: - advocating for greater support of horticulture for development initiatives worldwide; connecting and informing the diverse and dispersed community of horticulture for development professionals; coaching funded research projects addressing key constraints to achieving the GlobalHort mission and building the indigenous human capacity required to support smallholders investing in horticultural enterprises.

Hardy Plant Society – www.hardy-plant.org.uk – formed in 1957 to encourage the growing of hardy perennials, this society has a regional group structure that gives direct support to its members. An excellent organisation to help you source those must have plants and to gain knowledge on cultivation and propagation.

Incredible Edible – www.incredibleediblenetwork.org.uk – this exciting global network, started by two very enthusiastic ladies in Todmorden, West Yorkshire in 2008, is trying to get groups of people in every community to contribute to the well-being of their neighbourhood. This includes the growing and sharing of food in public and private situations. The concept and the reality are more than Pamela Warhurst and Mary Clear could have imagined in their wildest dreams when they first started but it is now a global phenomenon that we should all adopt.

The Invertebrate Conservation Trust – www.buglife.org.uk – an organisation whose sole purpose is to help conserve invertebrates through education and direct activities. With over 40,000 invertebrates recognised in the UK, they have their work cut out. An excellent website.

Kew Gardens – www.kew.org - as one of the world's most important Botanic Gardens, The Royal Botanic Gardens Kew is at the forefront of plant conservation and education globally with 25% of the world's wild plants conserved in the Millennium Seed Bank at Wakehurst Place, let alone the expertise that is carried across the planet by the staff to assist others in understanding the importance of plant conservation.

Kirkwood Hospice – www.kirkwoodhospice.co.uk – this well-established adult hospice, based in Huddersfield, with 25 + years of care behind it, provides hospice and home care to adults and their families in the Huddersfield area.

Meteorological Office – www.metoffice.gov.uk - we all watch the forecasts every day and listen to the weather people giving us the details that they think we ought to know. Visit the Met. Office website and find out a whole lot more about our weather and climate. Indicators of weather conditions of up to 10 days in advance might save some of your precious plants from the ravages of weather extremes. There is an excellent app for those with i-phones.

National Garden Scheme – www.ngs.org.uk – with more than 3500 gardens across Britain to visit and all those opportunities to rob ideas from others, who could ask for anything more. In addition, many have plant stalls and the entry charges are donated to a wide variety of charities. A new 'Yellow Book' is published each spring with the details of each garden, allowing us to plan trips out during the spring, summer and autumn, to enjoy the efforts of others and to benefit from their hard work and dedication. The listings are divided into counties to allow for easier reference.

National Plant Monitoring Scheme – www.npms.org.uk – this is a new (2018) habitat-based plant monitoring scheme designed to collect data, with the help of volunteers all over the UK, on wild plant abundance and diversity. Anyone wishing to be involved should contact the NPMS through their website.

National Society of Allotment and Leisure Gardeners – www.nsalg.org.uk – established in 1930, this umbrella organisation provides support and advice to anyone who is involved in allotmenteering, whether it be cultural or legal. A network of regional groups helps to maintain the societies work at a local level. The website is extensive and worthy of a visit. Members get a variety of benefits. There is a similar organisation for Scotland - visit www. sags.org.uk .

National Trust – www.nationaltrust.org.uk - this charitable institution probably needs little introduction to anyone but visit their website to gain an insight into their works, both current and historically. From a pure gardening perspective, the NT has done much in recent years to restore and care for some important historical gardens. Download the 2009 'Space to Grow' report from the National Trust website to gain a better understanding of how they are working to help us all value our gardening space.

National Vegetable Society – www.nvsuk.org.uk – an umbrella organisation that supports, advises and encourages those that enjoy the growing, showing and eating of home-grown vegetables. Details of shows, regional and local groups and lots of advice.

Northern Fruit Group – www.northernfruitgroup.com – a members led organisation, set up to support and help growers, both professional and amateur, to grow fruit in a northern climate. They usually have a stand at the Great Yorkshire Show in July (www. greatyorkshireshow.co.uk) and the Harrogate Flower Shows in April and September (www. flowershow.org.uk) for those that prefer face to face advice.

North of England Horticultural Society – www.flowershow.org.uk – organisers of the Harrogate Spring and Autumn flower shows.

Permaculture Association – www.permaculture.org.uk – for those that are able and willing, permaculture is more than just environmentally friendly gardening – it is a complete way of life and has a growing army of dedicated followers across the planet. Visit the website to get an overview of the concept and the work of this charitable organisation.

Pesticide Safety Directorate – www.hse.gov.uk – a British Government's website that allows you to research chemicals for the garden, if you feel that you must use them, and to guide you through the complex problem of disposing of unwanted chemicals when you finally realise that you can manage without them! The site also keeps us up-to-date with changes of approval for pesticides.

Plant Heritage – www.plantheritage.com / www.nccpg.com – formed in 1978, the NCCPG, as it was originally called, has county-based groups, including a Yorkshire based one, that hold national collections of plants, with the aid of dedicated organisations and individuals. Its purpose is to conserve plant species and cultivars, many of which are under threat or have been lost to general cultivation.

Plantlife – www.plantlife.org.uk – a members-based charity, started in 1989, that concentrates its efforts on nature's wild plants. It owns 23 nature reserves across Britain, covering 1,800 hectares, and runs campaigns and projects to raise the profile of our wild plants and the need to conserve them and their habitats.

Plant List – www.theplantlist.org – a recent addition to the army of valuable websites for gardeners, nurserymen and women, botanists, scientists and others. With over 1 million species on the list and 620 family names as well as over 16,000 Genera, this new resource will help to ensure that we can all use the most up-to-date scientific names for our plants.

It identifies names that have been fully accepted and also any synonyms that may have been considered in the past, allowing you to search via either of these routes. It have been a collaborative effort between the Royal Botanic Gardens Kew and the Missouri Botanic Gardens with others contributing to the process.

Plantwise – www.plantwise.org – created by Commonwealth Agricultural Bureaux International (CABI) in 2011, this website provides growers and farmers with details on pests, diseases and weeds to help them care for their crops more affectively. And much more…

Royal Entomological Society – www.royalensoc.co.uk – a society devoted to the promotion and development of entomological science. It organises National Insect Week (www.nationalinsectweek.co.uk) every two years to help encourage us all to take a greater interest in and have a greater understanding of the incredible and complex world of insects.

Royal Horticultural Society – www.rhs.org.uk – the leading gardening charity, with over 200 years of experience to hand on to gardeners of all classes and creeds. With four gardens to trial, demonstrate and educate as well as vast information resources, it is a premier stimulator of gardening techniques and plants, with a worldwide reputation. The web site is an encyclopaedia of up-to-date and valuable information and advice. Download the RHS's 2011 Gardening Matters: Urban Gardens report to see some of the issues that those of us living and gardening in urban environments face in the 21st Century. Visit RHS Garden Harlow Carr near Harrogate (www.rhs.org.uk/harlowcarr) for its wonderful gardens and some excellent events throughout the year.

Royal Society for the Protection of Birds – www.rspb.org.uk – this charity probably doesn't need any introduction but, along with its sister organisation, the British Trust for Ornithology (www.bto.org) , the RSPB provides some of the best support for our wild bird populations, both resident and migratory, through its network of reserves, support groups and educational and research work.

Soil Association – www.soilassociation.org – this membership based charity's main focus is on the production of healthy, humane and sustainable food production, farming and land use. It certificates organic producers, giving them the right to use the Soil Association logo on their products and it lobbies government on a wide range of food related issues. A worthy website for all of us.

The British Soil Society – www.soils.org.uk – for all things pedological, the BSS is a society formed to advance the understanding of soil science. Interesting website.

The Cottage Garden Society – www.thecgs.org.uk – an excellent website that allows you access to the society and its work. This is a member led organisation with a quarterly magazine, local and regional groups, national and regional events, all focussed on the core principles of cottage gardens, gardening and plants.

The Orchard Project – www.theorchardproject.org.uk – a National Charity dedicated to the creation, restoration and celebration of community orchards. A very worthy charity doing excellent work in Yorkshire and beyond.

The Tree Council – www.treecouncil.org.uk – this membership based organisation has been running since 1974, on the back of the 1973 'Plant a tree in 73' campaign and started National Tree Week in 1975. An excellent website and a very worthy organisation.

The Tree Register – www.treeregister.org – a register of some of the most valuable trees in the UK. At the time of publishing over 200,000 trees have been identified and registered. Trees may be ancient, rare, have important historic and botanical / environmental value. His Royal Highness the Prince of Wales is the organisations Patron.

UK Moths – www.ukmoths.org.uk – this comprehensive website allows visitors to view over 2000 photographs of moths from across Great Britain and Ireland – well worth a visit for those that find these mostly nocturnal creatures fascinating.

West Yorkshire Forget-me-not Childrens' Hospice – www.forgetmenotchild.co.uk - opened in Huddersfield in 2011, this purpose built Childrens' Hospice now provides services to the children and families of Kirklees, Calderdale and Wakefield Local Authorities areas.

Wild About Gardens – www.wildaboutgardens.org.uk - the combined resources of The Wildlife Trusts and the Royal Horticultural Society have been brought together to provide this superb website to help us learn more about how to use our gardens as wildlife habitats.

Wildlife Gardening Forum – www.wlgf.org – a charitable organisation with organisations and individual members. Conferences and newsletters help to keep members informed and allow the transfer of knowledge and understanding of this most complex of subjects. Worth joining up.

Woodland Trust – www.woodlandtrust.org.uk - a registered charity set up to help protect ancient trees, woodlands and forests and to advise and work with government, schools and other organisations to protect and develop the tree stock of the UK.

Worldwide Opportunities on Organic Farms – www.wwoof.org.uk - for organic farmers and those who want to learn more and to practice organic crop production and farming, this worldwide system allows them to connect and for individuals to join organic farmers and growers for days, weeks or months, with both parties benefitting – a perfect symbiotic relationship.

Appendix 3

Weeds for Each Garden Situation and How to Control Them

I HAVE INCLUDED the common names for these weeds to assist readers in their searches. The two keys are used in combination to give as complete a picture of the weeds and their potential control methods as possible. Refer to Chapter 7 for more thoughts on the management of these garden invaders. The list is not definitive but includes some of the worst offenders. If you have to use herbicides as a last resort, please ensure that you check that the products are approved for current use by visiting www.pesticides.gov.uk .

If you insist on using selective herbicides on lawns, do not put the grass clippings onto your compost heap or in the green waste recycling systems as the chemicals may come back to you in the form of green waste potting composts and damage some of your precious garden plants and vegetables, particularly those in the Solanaceae family.

Of course, many of the plants that us humans choose to call weeds are wildflowers in the wrong place and so some of us may be able to accept them into our gardens as part of the diverse mix of plants that wildlife gardening requires to be wholly successful. Many of the seeds of these plants will have been blown in on then wind, brought in by us as we import plants into our garden and, commonly, the seeds will come in through birds and mammals bringing them in in their faeces and on their feathers or fir, without us ever being aware of it, until a wildflower or weed appears!

KEY:

Control methods:

C	use an approved contact herbicide.
F	fork out at any time of the year.
H	hoe in warm, dry weather.
M	weed suppressed by mulching.
R	use an approved residual herbicide.
S	use an approved selective herbicide.
SSB	stale seed bed technique (see Chapter 7).
T	use an approved translocated herbicide.

Growth habit:

AE	Annual / ephemeral lifecycle.
Bi	Biennial lifecycle.
BT	bulbous or tuberous.
Fib	Fibrous rooted.
For	Foreign invader.
P	Perennial lifecycle.
RHI	Rhizomatous.
ST	Stoloniferous.
Tap	tap-rooted.

Flower Borders

Capsella bursa-pastoris (Shepherds Purse) – C, H, M, R, AE, Fib;
Cardamine hirsuta (Hairy Bittercress) – C, H, M, R, AE, Fib;
Chenopodium album (Fat hen) – C, H, M, R, AE, Fib;
Fumaria officinalis (Common fumitory) – C, H, M, R, AE, Fib;
Sagina procumbens (Procumbent pearlwort) – C, H, M, R, P, Fib;
Stellaria media (Chickweed) - C, H, M, AE, Fib;
Urtica urens (Annual nettle) – C, H, M, AE, Fib.

Lawns

Achillea millifolium (Yarrow) – S, Fib, P;
Bellis perennis (Diasy) – F, S, Fib, P;
Holcus lanatus (Yorkshire fog) – F, S, Fib, P;
Luzula campestris (Field wood-rush) – Fib, P;
Medicago lupulina (Black medick) – S, AE, Fib, P, ST;
Plantago major (Greater plantain) – S, Fib, P;
Sagina procumbens (Procumbent pearlwort) – C, H, M, R, Fib, P;
Taraxicum officinale (Dandelion) – F, S, P, T, Tap;
Trifolium repens (White clover) – S, Fib, P, ST.

Paths

Poa annua (Annual meadow grass) – C, F, T, AE, Fib;
Sedum acre (Biting stonecrop) – H, T, P, Fib;
Sagina procumbens (Procumbent pearlwort) – C, H, M, R, Fib, P;
Taraxicum officinale (Dandelion) – F,S,P,T.

Shrub Borders

Aegopodium podagraria (Ground elder) – F, T, P, RHI;
Circaea luetiana (Enchanters Nightshade) – F, T, P, ST;
Elymus repens (Couch grass) – F, T, P, RHI;
Chamaenerion angustifolium (Rosebay willowherb) – F, T, P, RHI;
Chamaenerion montanum (Broad-leaved willowherb) – F, H, T, Fib, P;
Galium aparine (Cleavers) – C, F, H, M, A, Bi, Fib;
Impatiens glandulifera (Himalayan balsam) – C, F, H, M, R, T, AE, Fib, For;
Oxalis acetosella (Wood sorrel) – F, H, R, T, Fib, P, ST;
Ranunculus ficaria (Lesser celandine) – F, T, BT, P;
Rubus fruticosus (Bramble) – F, T, Fib, P;
Rumex obtusifolius (Broad-leaved dock) – F, R, T, P, Tap;
Taraxicum officinale (Dandelion) – F, S, P, T, Tap;
Vicia sepium (Bush vetch) – F, R, T, P, ST;
Viola riviniana (Common dog violet) – F, H, R, T, Fib, P, ST.

Uncultivated / Neglected Areas

Calystegia sylvatica (Great bindweed) – F, T, P, RHI;
Cirsium arvense (Creeping thistle) – F, T, P, RHI;
Elymus repens (Couch grass) – F, T, P, RHI;

Fallopia japonica (Japanese knotweed) – F, T, For, P, RHI;
Galium aparine (Cleavers) – C, F, H, M, A, Bi, Fib;
Impatiens glandulifera (Himalayan balsam) – C, F, H, M, R, T, AE, Fib, For;
Pteridium aquilinum (Bracken) – F, T, P, RHI;
Rubus fruticosus (Bramble) – F, T, Fib, P;
Senecio jacobaea (Ragwort) – F, T, Bi, Fib;
Urticia dioica (Nettle) – F, R, T, Fib, P, ST;
Persicaria aviculare (Knotgrass) – C, F, H, T, AE, F.

VEGETABLE GARDENS

Capsella bursa-pastoris (Shepherds Purse) – C, H, M, SSB, AE, Fib; *Cardamine hirsuta* (Hairy Bittercress) – C, H, M, SSB, AE, Fib; *Chenopodium album* (Fat hen) – C, H, M, SSB, AE, Fib;
Elymus repens (Couch grass) – F, T, P, RHI;
Equisetum arvense (Horsetail) – F, T, P, RHI;
Fumaria officinalis (Common fumitory) – C, H, M, SSB, AE, Fib;
Sagina procumbens (Procumbent pearlwort) – C, H, M, SSB, P, Fib;
Sinapsis arvensis (Charlock) – C, H, M, SSB, AE, Fib;
Stellaria media (Chickweed) - C, H, M, SSB, AE, Fib;
Taraxicum officinale (Dandelion) – F, SSB, P, T, Tap;
Urticia dioica (Nettle) – F, R, T, Fib, P, ST;
Urtica urens (Annual nettle) – C, H, M, SSB, AE, Fib.

AQUATIC ENVIRONMENTS (USE OF HERBICIDES IN AQUATIC ENVIRONMENTS IS STRICTLY CONTROLLED)

Crassula helmsii (Australian Swamp Stonecrop) – T, Fib, For, P.
Fallopia japonica (Japanese Knotweed) – T, For, P, Rhi.
Heracleum mantagazzianum (Giant Hogweed) - F, T, Fib, For, P, Tap.
Hydrocotyle ranunculoides (Floating pennywort) – T, Fib, For, P.
Impatiens glandulifera (Himalayan Balsam) – F, H, T, A, F, For.
Ludwigia spps (Creeping water primrose) – T, For, P, ST.
Myriophyllum aquaticum (Parrot's feather) – T, Fib, For, P.

Appendix 4

Glossary
of Terms

LIKE MOST PROFESSIONS, horticulture is cluttered with a confusing array of words not always in common use in our everyday world. This appendix is intended to help the reader decipher some of these terms so that it makes the understanding of, if not the reading of this and other horticulturally related books, a little easier.

There are two blank pages at the end of this appendix for you to add your own terms and definitions as and when you come across them.

Abiota – a generic term for anything that is non-living. See **biota.**

Acaricide – a substance specifically designed to control Arachnid pests.

Acid - this refers to a liquid whose **pH** measurement is between 0 and 7 on the pH scale. See **alkaline**.

Aerobic – conditions that have available oxygen for normal life processes. See **anaerobic.**

Algae – simple unicellular or multicellular plants that lack any true vascular system and are not differentiated into leaves, roots or stems. See **lichen.**

Algaecide – any manufactured product for the control of algae.

Alkaline – this refers to a liquid whose **pH** measurement is between 7 and 14 on the pH scale. See **acid.**

Allelopathy – the science of organisms exuding biochemicals into the growing environment to prevent other organisms from growing and surviving. See **bio-fumigants.**

Amphibian – a creature that can survive out of water but that requires a water source to complete its breeding cycle. Examples include frogs, newts and toads.

Anaerobic – conditions that do not have available oxygen for normal life processes. See **aerobic.**

Angiosperm – literally means covered seed. A group of plants that contains **dicotyledons** and **monocotyledons**. These are the vast majority of plants that we know in our garden. It does not include **Gymnosperms, ferns, mosses, algae, liverworts, lichen** or **fungi.**

Annual – a plant that completes a full life cycle, from seed to seed, in one growing season. An example of this is *Papaver rhoeas* (Flanders poppy). See **biennial, ephemeral, half-hardy, hardy** and **perennial.**

Apical dominance – showing itself as a strong leading shoot that has the majority of the growth hormones. See **lateral, leader** and **spur**.

Apiculture – the study and care of honey bees.

Aquatic plant – a plant that requires to be immersed in water for the whole of its life cycle. They may be wholly or partly submerged, marginal or floating.

Arboretum – a garden whose main displays are trees of either ornamental or commercial value. See **pinetum**.

Arboriculturist – a person who cares for trees – commonly known as a tree surgeon.

Arid – a climate in which desert and semi-desert species of plants can survive. Described as being global. Full to partial seasonal variations. See **Mediterranean, Polar, sub-tropical, temperate** and **tropical.**

AYR – this is the abbreviation for all year round. Sometimes used for plants such as cut-flower and pot grown Chrysanthemums.

Bactericide – manufactured products for the control of bacteria.

Bacterium – the largest group of micro-organisms in the world living in every part of our world. Some are very destructive diseases but most are beneficial. Estimates of 40 million to every gram of every healthy garden soil gives us an idea of their numbers on a global scale.

Base dressing – the application of a fertilizer or bulky organic material to an area of soil prior to planting or sowing. See **top dressing**.

Beaufort wind force scale – a measurement of wind speed normally accepted as a 1-12 scale up to hurricane force. Named after Francis Beaufort in the early 19th century and originally used by mariners.

Bed – any area of planting that is surrounded by lawns or paths. See **border**.

Bed rock - the underlying rock from which sub-soil and topsoil are developed. See **sub-soil** and **topsoil.**

Biennial – a plant that completes a full life cycle over two growing seasons. An example of this is *Digitalis* (foxglove). See **annual, ephemeral** and **perennial**.

Biodigestion – the disposal of human food waste using anaerobic bacteria, with the benefit of CO_2 and Methane being given off as by-products. Now being used widely in industry and for glasshouse heating.

Biodynamics – the understanding and adaptation of growing techniques in tune with weather, seasonal, solar, lunar and earth cycles.

Biofumigant – using the principles of **Allelopathy,** the use of plants to discourage or kill other living organisms in a growing environment.

Biology – the scientific study of all living organisms.

Biological control – the use of naturally occurring and managed parasites, pathogens and predators to help reduce disease, pest and weed attacks. See **Chemical control, Cultural control** and **Physical control**.

Biopesticide – a contraction of biological pesticide. Any micro-organism or natural product that can be applied to crops for the control / reduction of pests and diseases. This includes all currently available biological control mechanisms – fungi, insect **predators**

and **parasites**, both naturally occurring in the open garden and the 'manufactured' types available commercially.

Biophilia – a relatively new term that is being used by many as an umbrella word to cover all things environmental – some Cities are using the term to help them connect all their activities together in an environmentally friendly way. Oslo is apparently well on the way and Birmingham (UK) is now working towards a biophilic status.

Biota – a generic term for any living organisms. See **abiota**

Border – any area of planting that can only be seen from one main side. Usually backed by fences, walls or hedges. See **bed**.

Botanist – a person who studies the structure of plants and the processes that go on in those plants.

Bulb – a compressed stem (basal plate) with fleshy leaves or scales attached. *Alliums* (Onions) and *Narcissi* are both common examples. See also **corm, rhizome, stolon** and **tuber**.

Calcareous – a term used to describe any soil that is alkaline and has been formed over limestone or chalk.

Calcicole – a plant that has a preference for alkaline soils.

Calcifuge – a plant that does not cope well when there are high levels of Calcium in the soil.

Carbon cycle – a natural cycle of the carbon element being stored in plants and animals as they consume food and the release of that carbon as plants and animals defecate and decompose. Agents include **fungi** and humans that help to process carbon rich plant and animal material.

Carnivore – a creature whose diet is exclusively the fresh of another creature. See **herbivore** and **omnivore**.

Chemical control – the use of naturally occurring and manufactured compounds for the control of diseases, pests and weeds. See **Biological control, Cultural control** and **Physical Control**.

Clay – flat mineral particles that form the heaviest soils with bad drainage but good nutrient retention. Particle size is smaller than silt. See **sand** and **silt**.

Climbers – plants that have evolved an adaptation in their growing habits and structure to be able to climb up other plants – adventitious roots, hooks, sucker pads, tendrils and twisting stems are examples.

Coir – a waste product from the coconut industry that can be used as a potting compost. Seen by some a substitute for peat.

Companion planting – the use of one or more plants to benefit and protect others. Examples include the use of Nitrogen fixing plants and **biofumigant** plants. See **sacrificial planting**.

Cordon – a technique of growing trees and shrubs where the plant is grown at a 45° angle to the vertical. Trees and shrubs are grown against a wall or trained on posts and wires. See **espalier** and **fan**.

Corm – a compressed stem with a central bud. True corms replace themselves every year whilst the parent plant is growing. Examples include *Crocus* and *Gladioli*. See also **bulb, rhizome, stolon** and **tuber**.

Crepuscular – a creature that comes out at dawn or dusk. See **diurnal** and **nocturnal**.

Crop rotation – an ancient farming technique of rotating groups of crops on different plots of land to help reduce the build up of pests and diseases and to ensure that each plot has the right soil conditions for the next crop, sometimes based on what the previous crop has extracted from the soil or left behind. The length of the rotation can vary from 3 to 5 years. See **fallow**.

Cross-pollination – the transfer of pollen from one plant to another. See **pollination** and **self-pollination**.

Cultural control – the use of good horticultural practices to reduce the incidence of pest, disease, weed and physiological disorder attacks on our plants. This may include correct techniques and timing for propagation and pruning. It includes the selection of correct growing techniques for plants with known resistance to problems. See **Biological control, Chemical control** and **Physical control.**

Cultivar – a variation on a plant **species** created by human intervention. May be called a hybrid and is correctly written as 'Kelvedon Wonder' for example.

Deciduous - woody plants that shed their foliage at the end of their growing season.

Deficiency – a name given to conditions in plants and soils that are lacking in one or more essential nutrients. Common examples include Nitrogen, Calcium, Magnesium and Potassium deficiencies. Symptoms of these deficiencies are usually very distinctive.

Dendrology – the study of trees. A **dendrologist** is a person who studies trees. E.G. *Rhodo**dendron*** = Rose tree.

Detritus – debris that builds up from inorganic and organic waste.

Dicotyledon – plants that produce two seed leaves (cotyledons) either within the seed (**hypogeal**) or when the seedling emerges (**epigeal**).

Dioecious – plants that produce male and female flowers but on two separate plants. See **hermaphrodite** and **monoecious**. An example of this is *Ilex* (Holly).

Disease – any abnormal condition affecting the body of an organism – **fungi, bacteria** and **viruses** are the common causes of these conditions.

Disorder – the result of adverse conditions other than pest or disease damage affecting plant growth. Frost, wind, drought, shade and low nutrients levels are all examples of the causes of the disorders. May be known as **physiological disorders** and are **abiotic.**

Diurnal - a creature that carries out its normal activities during the hours of daylight. See **crepuscular** and **nocturnal**.

Drill – a shallow trench in soil into which seeds are sown. The depth of the drill is determined by the size of the seed being sown.

Ecology – the study of the relationship that living organisms have with their surroundings and the other living organisms that may interact with them.

Elements – substances that are distinguished by their atomic number that cannot be broken down into more fundamental substances. EG. Nitrogen (N). See **fertilisers** and **minerals.**

Entomology – the scientific study of insects. See **mycology** and **pathology**.

Ephemeral – a plant that completes a full life cycle, from seed to seed, more than once in a growing season. An example of this is the weed *Cardamine hirsuta* (Hairy Bittercress). See **annual, biennial** and **perennial**.

Epicormic – used to describe a shoot from the trunk of a tree.

Epigeal - the germination of a seed where the seed leaf / leaves are brought above soil. See **Hypogeal.**

Epiphyte – a plant that grows on another plant but does not necessarily **parasitize** or **predate** upon it. See **halophyte**, **lithophyte** and **xerophyte.**

Espalier – a style of growing of trees or shrubs where the lateral branches are trained out horizontally from a main trunk, with a given distance between each lateral. Trees and shrubs are grown against a wall or trained on posts and wires. See **cordon** and **fan.**

Ethology – the study of animal behaviour.

Etiolation – the effect of growing plants in reduced light conditions where leaf size is reduced, internodal stem length is increased and flowering potential is reduced.

Eugenics – the improvement of a race of animals or plants by breeding out and weeding out the undesirable traits.

Evergreen – usually but not exclusively plants that retain their leaves throughout the year, only discarding some of the older ones at the start of their new growing season. See **deciduous.**

Evolution - is the change in the inherited characteristics of biological populations over successive generations. In the garden this may be the gradual development or deterioration of one or all of the garden features.

F1 Hybrid – a plant that is created by the first-generation cross between two known parents.

F2 Hybrid – a plant that is created by self-pollination or inter-pollination of the F1 generation.

Fallow – a term to describe the process of leaving an area of land uncultivated and un-cropped for a period of time. This may be done to improve soil structure or to eradicate certain pests, diseases or weeds. See **crop rotation.**

Family – a group of **Genus** that all have some physical and genetic similarities. E.G. Rosaceae.

Fan – a technique of growing trees and shrubs where the laterals are trained out in a fan shape from the main short trunk. Trees and shrubs are grown against a wall or trained on posts and wires. See **cordon** and **espalier.**

Fasciation – a physiological disorder of some plants where the tips of leading shoots and laterals appear flattened.

Fastigiate – a term to describe trees or shrubs that have a columnar or pencil shape.

Feathered whip – a two to four year old seedling or grafted tree that has some lateral shoots. See **whip.**

Ferns – a group of primitive plants belonging to the division of the plant world known as Pteridophyta. They are commonly herbaceous but some grow to the size of trees.

Fertiliser – **inorganic** or **organic** material that can be added to the soil to supply one or more plant nutrients. May be dry powder or granule or a concentrated liquid for dilution. May be slow or quick release. May be compound (more than one element) or may be simple (one main element). See **elements** and **minerals.**

Flocculation – a term used to describe the joining of soil particles into larger aggregates or crumbs by the addition of lime. Particularly affective for heavy clay soils. See **clay**.

Food web – the interrelationship of living organisms to one another.

Forestry – the commercial production of timber. See **Sylviculture**.

Fungus – a group of organisms, completely separate to plants, animals and **bacteria** that may be **saprophytic** or **parasitic**. It includes yeasts, moulds and mushrooms / toadstools.

Fungicide – any manufactured or natural product for the control of fungi.

FYM – this is the abbreviation for farmyard manure. See **Green Manure.**

Genus – a group of **species** that all have some physical and genetic similarities. E.G. *Cotoneaster*. Sometimes able to cross-breed with other Genus in the Family. E.G. *Cupressus x leylandii*.

Geology – the study of rocks. See **pedology** and **topography.**

Geotropism – the movement of a plant in response to gravity – this can be negative or positive. See **phototropism** and **tropism**.

Graft – the union of a **rootstock** and a **scion**, usually without roots, to form a new known plant. See **scion** and **rootstock.**

Green manure – plants grown specifically to be dug into the soil before they reach maturity to add easily decomposed nitrogenous organic matter to the soil. See **FYM.**

Gymnosperm – literally means naked seed. A group of plants that includes conifers and, in evolutionary terms is older than **Angiosperms.**

Habitat – literally a place to live. In the garden this refers to both plants and creatures and the most suitable habitats for them.

Half-hardy – a plant that requires some glasshouse protection during the autumn, winter and spring months. See **annual, hardy** and **perennial.**

Halophyte – a plant adapted to surviving in very saline soil conditions. See **epiphyte, lithophyte** and **xerophyte.**

Hardy – a plant that can survive its full life cycle outdoors. See **annual, half-hardy** and **perennial.**

Herb – any plant that has aromatic, culinary or medicinal / pharmaceutical properties.

Herbaceous – plants that are not naturally capable of producing woody material. They may be **annual, biennial** or **perennial** and may show **evergreen** tendencies in some perennials.

Herbicide – any manufactured chemical for the control of weeds.

Herbivore – a creature whose diet is exclusively vegetarian. See **carnivore** and **omnivore.**

Hermaphrodite – a plant that has male and female flower parts within the same flower or a creature such as a slug or worm that has both female and male reproductive organs. An example of this is *Rosa* (rose).

Honeydew – the sticky, sugary liquid waste from sap sucking insects such as aphids and scale insects.

Humus – a sticky material left after all decomposition of organic matter has finished that helps soil particles to bind together.

Hydrotropism – a plants positive or negative response to water. Often associated with a plants root system. See **geotropism, phototropism** and **tropism.**

Hypogeal – the germination of a seed where the seed leaf / leaves remain below soil level. See **Epigeal**.

Inorganic – any material that is not of biological origin. See **organic.**

Insecticide – any manufactured or naturally occurring material for the control of the broader world of insects.

Invertebrate – any creature that does not have a backbone or spinal column. See **vertebrate.**

Lateral – any side shoot or branch growing from a main stem. See **leader** and **spur.**

Leader – a shoot that shows dominance over others. See **apical dominance, lateral** and **spur.**

Lithophyte – a plant adapted to growing on rocks. See **epiphyte, halophyte** and **xerophyte.**

Lichen – a composite organism formed by a **symbiotic** relationship between a **fungus** and a photosynthetic **alga** or **bacterium.**

Liverwort – a simple plant belonging to the Division of Bryophyta that also includes **moss.**

Marscesence – the retention of leaves on **deciduous** plants overwinter. E.G. *Carpinus* and *Fagus.*

Mediterranean – a climate in which Mediterranean species of plants can survive. Described as being outside the Tropics of Cancer and Capricorn. Full seasonal variations. See **arid, Polar, sub-tropical, temperate** and **tropical.**

Meteorology – the scientific study of climate and weather.

Microclimate – the conditions of light, moisture, shade and temperature etc that may be found in garden environments and which are different in some way to the surrounding area. See **temperature zones.**

Mineral – a naturally occurring inorganic, solid material with a distinct chemical formula. Some of these form the basic ingredients of soil. EG. Fluorite, Gold. See **elements.**

Molluscicide – any manufactured product for the control of slugs and snails.

Monocotyledons - plants that produce one seed leaf (cotyledon) either within the seed (**hypogeal**) or when the seedling emerges (**epigeal**). See **dicotyledons.**

Monoculture – the growing of one crop on a large scale. See **Polyculture.**

Monoecious – plants that produce both male and female flowers on one plant but separately. See **dioecious** and **hermaphrodite.** An example of this is *Begonia.*

Monophagous – a creature that feeds on one specific plant. EG. Gooseberry sawfly. See **Oligophagous** and **Polyphagous.**

Moss – primitive non-flowering plants that belong to the Division Bryophyta. See **liverworts.**

Mycology – the scientific study of fungi. See **entomology** and **pathology.**

Mycorrhiza – literally it means fungal root. These are microscopic fungi that attach themselves to the roots of plants and help the plant to absorb water and nutrients. The relationship is said to be **symbiotic.**

Myrmecology – the scientific study of ants.

Nitrogen cycle – a natural cycle of the Nitrogen element from the atmospheric Nitrogen gas into soil and plants and back to the atmosphere as plants decompose and animals urinate and defecate. Agents such as **bacteria**, **fungi** and precipitation help in the movement of Nitrogen from one form to another round the cycle.

Nocturnal – a creature that carries out its normal activities during the hours of darkness. See **crepuscular** and **diurnal**.

Nutrients – a range of major, minor and trace elements necessary to maintain healthy plant growth. See **nutrient deficiency.** Examples: Nitrogen (N), Phosphate (P), Potassium (K), Magnesium (Mg), Calcium (Ca), Iron (Fe).

Nutrient deficiency – the lack of one or more elements in the soil or the plant that adversely affects the plant's growth and productivity. See **nutrients.**

Oligophagous – a creature that feeds on a limited range of plants, often from the same plant family. EG. Large Cabbage White Butterfly. See **Monophagous** and **Polyphagous**.

Omnivore – a creature whose diet is a mixture of flesh and vegetative matter. See **carnivore** and **herbivore**.

Organic – any material that is of biological origin. See **inorganic**.

Ornithology – the scientific study of birds.

Parasite – a creature, plant or other organism that invades the body of another creature or plant, taking goodness from the host. See **predator** and **saprophyte**.

Parthenocarpy – the development of a fruit without any prior pollination or fertilisation. An example of this is *Cucumis sativus* (Cucumber).

Parthenogenesis – the reproductive method used by some of our common pests such as aphids. It is the development of an embryo inside the female from an unfertilized egg.

Pathology – the scientific study and diagnosis of pests, diseases and disorders. See **entomology** and **mycology**.

Pedology – the scientific study of soils. See **geology** and **topography**.

Perennial – a plant that survives for more than two growing seasons. An example of this is *Quercus* (oak). See **annual, biennial** and **ephemeral**.

Periodic table – a numeric system of identifying elements. EG. H (Hydrogen) is 1 on the table. See **elements** and **minerals**.

Permaculture – the growing of plants in a way that minimises the disturbance of natural processes and understands the balance of nature.

Pesticide – a generic term covering all organic and inorganic substances / organisms used for the control of pests, diseases and weeds. See **acaricide, algaecide, bactericide, biopesticide, biofumigant, fungicide, herbicide, insecticide, molluscicide** and **rodenticide,**

pH scale – the measurement of the **acidity** or **alkalinity** of a substance using a 0–14 scales. 7 is assumed to be neutral point on the scale. The scale is logarithmic and so each point up or down the scale measures 10 times more or less acidic or alkaline!

Phenology – the study of the times of recurring natural phenomena in relation to climatic and seasonal changes.

Photoperiodism – a physiological reaction of organisms to the length of day and night. Short day plants flower as the day length shortens after the summer solstice. Long day plants flower after the winter solstice.

Photosynthesis – the process by which complex sugars and starches (carbohydrates) are produced by plants. Sunlight, chlorophyll, Carbon dioxide and water are the essential agents.

Phototropism – the movement of a plant in response to a light source. See **geotropism, hydrotropism** and **tropism.**

Physical control – the use of physical barriers to prevent attack from diseases, pests or weeds and the physical removal of these when they occur. See **Biological control, Chemical control** and **Cultural control.**

Pinetum – a garden that collects, grows, studies and displays plants that are broadly coniferous. See **arboretum.**

Polar – a climate in which arctic, sub-arctic and tundra species of plants can survive. Described as being north or south of temperate zones. Full seasonal variations. See **arid, Mediterranean, sub-tropical, temperate** and **tropical.**

Pollination – the process of pollen transfer from the anther of one flower to the stigma of another. See **cross-pollination** and **self-pollination**

Polyculture – the growing of many different plants in one situation on a small or large scale. See **monoculture.**

Polyphagous – a creature that feeds on a wide variety of plants. EG. Slugs and snails. See **Monophagous** and **Oligophagous.**

Predator – a creature that catches and consumes all or part of another creature. See **parasite** and **saprophyte.**

Relative humidity – the relationship between air temperature and the moisture held in it – measured by wet and dry bulb thermometers and hygrometers.

Rhizome – an underground stem that serves as a storage organ. Examples include bamboo and ginger. See also **bulb, corm, stolon** and **tuber.**

Rodenticide – any manufactured chemical for the control of rodents.

Root stock – the root and stem onto which is **grafted** or budded a **scion.**

Sacrificial planting – the use of one susceptible plant to protect others from pest or disease attack. An example is *Tropaeolum majus* as a sacrificial plant for brassicas against Cabbage White Butterfly attack. See **Companion planting.**

Sand – soil particles that are angular, giving sandy soils their free-draining feature and gritty feel. They vary in size from 2mm to 0.2mm. See **clay** and **silt.**

Saprophyte – a fungus that invades and consumes dead plant material. See **parasite** and **predator.**

Scion – a piece of plant material, not normally with its own roots, that is attached to a **root stock** to form a new plant.

Seed – the resulting organism from sexual activity in a flower. It may produce identical offspring (F1 hybrids) or natural variations from both parent flowers. See **Spore** and **Vegetative propagation.**

Self-pollination – the transfer of pollen within the same flower. See **cross-pollination** and **pollination**.

Semi-permeable – a structure, plant or membrane that allows a certain percentage of air or liquid to pass through it. E.G. Fences, fleece, landscape fabrics and hedges.

Silt – a soil particle that has been formed through movement in water, given them their round shape and their smooth feel. Soil in flood plains and river estuaries are often silty. Particle size is 0.2mm to 0.22mm - between clay and sand. See **clay** and **sand**.

Soil – a complex amalgam of various sizes of rock particles (**sand, silt** and **clay**), air, water, dissolved nutrients, organic matter and living organisms to form a medium in which plants can grow. See **geology, pedology, sub-soil** and **top soil**.

Species – a sub-division of **Genus**. Able to cross-breed with other species within the Genus. E.G. *Cotoneaster simonsii.*

Spore – the reproductive unit produced by fungi, mosses, liverworts etc. See **Seed** and **Vegetative reproduction.**

Spur – a short lateral that bears flowers and fruit. See **lateral** and **leader**.

Stevenson's screen – a **meteorological** piece of equipment to hold thermometers and stop them being affected by direct sunlight. Named after Sir Thomas Stevenson, a 19th Century Civil Engineer and father of Robert Louis Stevenson, the author.

Stolon – a horizontal stem. Examples include *Fragaria* and *Mentha*. See also **bulbs, corms, rhizomes** and **tubers**.

Sub-soil – a distinct layer of soil immediately below the top soil that is texturally identical but lacks organic matter and many living organisms. It is usually lighter in colour than the top soil. See **soil** and **top soil**.

Subterranean – literally the word means below soil.

Sub-tropical – a climate in which sub-tropical species of plants grow. Described as being between the Tropics of Cancer and Capricorn. Some seasonal variations. See **arid, Mediterranean, Polar, temperate** and **tropical.**

Sucker – a shoot that grows from a root.

Sylviculture – the study of trees for commercial gain – see **forestry**.

Symbiosis – a relationship between two living organisms that is mutually beneficial.

Taxonomist – a person who studies the scientific classification of organisms – **taxonomy**.

Temperate – a climate in which temperate species of plants can survive. Described as being outside the Tropics of Cancer and Capricorn. Full seasonal variations. See **arid, Mediterranean, Polar, sub-tropical** and **tropical.**

Temperature zones - a rather variable and often inaccurate method of identifying temperature ranges in which parts of the world sit and therefore in which only certain plants can survive. See **microclimates.**

Tilth – a well-prepared soil with a suitable sized crumb structure for the crop being planted or sown. A tilth can be fine, medium or coarse.

Top dressing - the application of fertilizers or bulky organic material to an existing crop. See **base dressing**.

Top soil – the upper most layer of soil that is usually darker in colour than the sub-soil from which it originates. It contains all the main ingredients of soil. See **soil** and **sub-soil**.

Topography – a description of the surface shapes and features of an area of land – the lie of the land! It may include historic features, vegetation, artificial features such as buildings, roads etc that draws a picture of an area. Details such as soil type, bedrock, drainage, rivers etc can be included in any description on the topography of an area. See **geology** and **pedology**.

Tropical – a climate in which tropical plants can grow – equal day and night length, high day and night temperatures and high rainfall. Few, if any, seasonal variations. Described as being between the Tropics of Cancer and Capricorn. See **Arid, Mediterranean, Polar, sub-tropical** and **temperate**.

Tropism – the movement of a plant in response to an outside stimulus. E.G. Light. See **geotropism, hydrotropism** and **phototropism**.

Tuber – a storage organ that may be an adapted root or stem. E.G. *Dahlia* – root tuber. *Solanum tuberosum* (potato) – stem tuber. See also **bulb, corm, rhizome** and **stolon**.

Vegetative propagation – the increase in numbers of plants by the use of vegetative material taken from a plant. Division and cuttings are examples. Resulting new plants are genetically identical to their parent plant (**Clones**). Known broadly as asexual propagation. See **Seed**.

Vertebrate – any creature that has a backbone or spinal column. See **invertebrate**.

Virus - an infectious agent that can only replicate itself in living cells of plants, animals, insects etc.

Viticulture – the growing of grape vines.

Water shoot – a vigorous, often vertical, shoot growing from the trunk or a branch of a tree or shrub. They are often weak, unproductive and prone to attack by pests or diseases.

Whip – a one or two year old seedling or grafted new tree without any **lateral shoots**. See **feathered whip**.

Xerophyte – a plant capable of surviving in extremely dry conditions. See **epiphyte, halophyte** and **lithophyte**.

Appendix 5

Poems to Enjoy

THROUGHOUT THE BOOK, either at the beginning of each Chapter or referred to during a Chapter or even included in a chapter, I have offered words of wisdom written by others, far more eminent than I and so, for those that enjoy poetry and reading, and have quiet moments to sit in their garden, I have reproduced some of the poems in full.

THE GLORY OF THE GARDEN (1911)

Our England is a garden that is full of stately views,
Of borders, beds and shrubberies and lawns and avenues,
With statues on the terraces and peacocks strutting by;
But the Glory of the Garden lies in more than meets the eye.

For where the old thick laurels grow, along the thin red wall,
You will find the tool- and potting-sheds which are the heart of all;
The cold-frames and the hot-houses, the dungpits and the tanks:
The rollers, carts and drain-pipes, with the barrows and the planks.

And there you'll see the gardeners, the men and 'prentice boys
Told off to do as they are bid and do it without noise;
For, except when seeds are planted and we shout to scare the birds,
The Glory of the Garden it abideth not in words.

And some can pot Begonias and some can bud a rose,
And some are hardly fit to trust with anything that grows;
But they can roll and trim the lawns and sift the sand and loam,
For the Glory of the Garden occupieth all who come.

Our England is a garden, and such gardens are not made
By singing:--"Oh, how beautiful!" and sitting in the shade,
While better men than we go out and start their working lives
At grubbing weeds from gravel-paths with broken dinner-knives.

There's not a pair of legs so thin, there's not a head so thick,
There's not a hand so weak and white, nor yet a heart so sick.
But it can find some needful job that's crying to be done,
For the Glory of the Garden glorifieth everyone.

Then seek your job with thankfulness and work till further orders,
If it's only netting strawberries or killing slugs on borders;
And when your back stops aching and your hands begin to harden,
You will find yourself a partner in the Glory of the Garden.

Oh, Adam was a gardener, and God who made him sees
That half a proper gardener's work is done upon his knees,
So when your work is finished, you can wash your hands and pray
For the Glory of the Garden, that it may not pass away!
And the Glory of the Garden it shall never pass away!

Rudyard Kipling (1865–1936)

THE NATURALIST'S SUMMER-EVENING WALK
TO THOMAS PENNANT, ESQUIRE

... equidem credo, quia sit divinitus illis
Ingenium. (For my part, I believe, because God has given them the talent)
Virg., Georg.

When day declining sheds a milder gleam,
What time the may-fly haunts the pool or stream;
When the still owl skims round the grassy mead,
What time the timorous hare limps forth to feed;
Then be the time to steal adown the vale,
And listen to the vagrant cuckoo's tale;
To hear the clamorous curlew call his mate,
Or the soft quail his tender pain relate;
To see the swallow sweep the dark'ning plain
Belated, to support her infant train;
To mark the swift in rapid giddy ring
Dash round the steeple, unsubdu'd of wing:
Amusive birds! -- say where your hid retreat
When the frost rages and the tempests beat;
Whence your return, by such nice instinct led,
When spring, soft season, lifts her bloomy head?
Such baffled searches mock man's prying pride,
The God of Nature is your secret guide!
While deep'ning shades obscure the face of day
To yonder bench leaf-shelter'd let us stray,
'Till blended objects fail the swimming sight,
And all the fading landscape sinks in night;
To hear the drowsy dorr come brushing by
With buzzing wing, or the shrill cricket cry;
To see the feeding bat glance through the wood;
To catch the distant falling of the flood;
While o'er the cliff th'awakened churn-owl hung
Through the still gloom protracts his chattering song;"
While high in air, and pois'd upon his wings,
Unseen, the soft, enamour'd woodlark sings:
These, Nature's works, the curious mind employ,
Inspire a soothing melancholy joy:
As fancy warms, a pleasing kind of pain
Steals o'er the cheek, and thrills the creeping vein!
Each rural sight, each sound, each smell, combine;
The tinkling sheep-bell, or the breath of kine;
The new-mown hay that scents the swelling breeze,
Or cottage-chimney smoking through the trees.

The chilling night-dews fall: away, retire;
For see, the glow-worm lights her amorous fire!
Thus, ere night's veil had half obscur'd the sky,
Th'impatient damsel hung her lamp on high:
True to the signal, by love's meteor led,
Leander hasten'd to his Hero's bed.

By: Rev. Gilbert White (1720–1793)

TIME TO STAND & STARE

What is this life if full of care
We have no time to stand and stare?
No time to stand beneath the boughs
And stare as long as sheep, or cows.
No time to see, when woods we pass,
Where squirrels hide their nuts in grass.
No time to see, in broad daylight,
Streams full of stars, like skies at night.
No time to turn at Beauty's glance,
And watch her feet, how they can dance.
No time to wait till her mouth can
Enrich that smile her eyes began.
A poor life this, if full of care,
We have no time to stand and stare.

William Henry Davies (1871–1940)

Appendix 6

Gardens Worthy of A Visit

THIS IS NOT an exhaustive list because, like all of us, there are a great many gardens that I have yet to hear of or visit, both here in Yorkshire and across the UK and abroad. However, the gardens that I have included are ones that, by personal experience or reliable recommendation, I feel able to offer the reader, to help enhance their horticultural understanding and appreciation as well as their attitude towards a more caring, environmentally friendly way of managing their small piece of Mother Nature's planet, let alone the wider world. There are a number of gardens listed that are outside the Yorkshire boundaries that are worthy of a day trip.

If you find a good garden to visit and learn from, don't keep it to yourself but pass it on to as many of your friends and associates as you can. Always check websites etc for opening times as these can vary.

Beningbrough Hall, York, YO30 1DD (www.nationaltrust.org.uk) – a large working walled garden with over 50 varieties of apples and pears to admire.

Biddolph Grange, Grange Road, Biddolph, Stoke-on-trent, ST8 7SD, (www.nationaltrust. org.uk) – a garden designed and laid out by James Bateman in the mid 1900s. Fascinating features like the China garden, the Stumpery and the Dahlia Border will give you ideas for your own gardens.

Bide-a-Wee Cottage Gardens, Morpeth, Northumberland, NE65 8PR (www.bideawee. co.uk) – a delightful quarry garden that shows lots of variations of aspect, topography, soil type and moisture. A good garden to learn from for those gardening in challenging situations.

Bluecoat Nurseries, Otley Road, Harrogate HG3 1QL (www.horticap.org) – a nursery, gardens and café established to provide support and training for adults with learning difficulties. A worthy visit to a worthy cause. Visit RHS Gardens Harlow Carr whilst you are there – a 5 minute walk!

Brodsworth Hall, Brodsworth, Doncaster, DN5 7XJ (www.english-heritage.org.uk) – an extensive mid 1800s house and garden that has been fully restored and is a worthy garden to visit.

The Dorothy Clive Garden, Market Drayton, Shropshire, TF9 4EU (www. dorothyclivegarden.co.uk) – another quarry garden to give you inspiration.

Dunham Massey, Altrincham, Cheshire, WA14 4SJ (www.nationaltrust.org.uk) – Britain's largest winter garden should inspire you to add winter to your gardening seasons.

Fountains Abbey and Studley Royal Water Gardens, Ripon, North Yorkshire, HG4 3DY (www.nationaltrust.org.uk) – now managed by the National Trust, these vast estates with their impressive buildings, gardens, deer park and vistas are a must have visit.

Harewood House and Gardens, Sandy Gate, Harewood, Leeds, LS17 9LG (www.harewood.org) – this vast estate (over 40 hectares of gardens) is an example of Capability Brown landscaping at its best. With additional gardens being added over the centuries, this is a fabulous day out.

Helmsley Walled Garden, Helmsley, North Yorkshire, YO62 5AH (www.helmsleywalledgarden.org.uk)–20 years on from the beginning of its new life in the 1990s, this garden should be on everyone's itinerary. You can visit Duncombe Park and the delightful town of Helmsley whilst you are there.

Himalayan Gardens and Sculpture Park, The Hutts, Grewelthorpe, Ripon, North Yorkshire, HG4 3DA (www.himalayangarden.com) – opened in 2005, this 20 acre garden is open from April to June and for a short period at the end of October each year and is laid out in the style of a Himalayan hillside, giving a naturalistic effect to the plantings of Magnolias and Rhododendrons with typical underplanting. Although slightly off the beaten track it is well worth the effort. Visit the National Trust's Fountains Abbey and Thorp Perrow Arboretum whilst you are in the area.

Horticap Harrogate (www.horticap.org) – a wonderful garden, nursery and cafe that supports adults with learning difficulties. Just round the corner from RHS Garden Harlow Carr.

Leeds City Parks – with Temple Newsam, Lotherton Hall and Roundhay Park as the main highlights, Leeds City Council have some of the best gardens and landscapes in Yorkshire managed by a local authority. Their new Arium nursery at Thorner Lane, Scarcroft, Leeds, LS14 3FB (www.theariumleeds.co.uk) is also a must do visit.

Littlethorpe Manor Gardens, Littlethorpe, Ripon, HG4 3LG, (www.littlethorpemanor.com) – a 4.5 hectare garden on the edge of the Ripon Canal with 1.6 hectares of formal gardens and 2.9 hectares of parkland.

Middlethorpe Hall, Bishopthorpe Road, York, YO23 2GB (www.middlethorpe.com www.nationaltrust.org.uk) – a Hotel, Restaurant and Spa close to the centre of York with stunning formal and informal gardens. The complex is a joint venture between Historic House Hotels Ltd and the National Trust.

National Gardens Scheme (www.yorkshire.com and www.ngs.org.uk) – with over 100 gardens opening their garden gates for this organisation across the year, there are some wonderful examples of public and private gardens for you to enjoy and to contribute to a variety of charities at the same time. For those with smart phones, there is an app that you can download. For those without that technology, there is a booklet with all the gardens detailed.

Ness Botanic Gardens, Neston, Wirral, CH64 4AY (www.nessgardens.org.uk) – this lesser known botanic garden is nowadays managed by the University of Liverpool and has some worthy garden features and plants to search out.

Newby Hall, Ripon, North Yorkshire, HG4 5AE (www.newbyhall.com) – a renowned garden and house, with the famous, long mirror herbaceous borders that run from the house to the River Ure. Lots to do for the whole family – look out for plant sales events, the Dolls House collection, Chippendale furniture and Teddy Bears!

Normanby Hall Country Park, Scunthorpe, DN15 9HU (www.northlincs.gov.uk/normanby) – the restored walled garden is an excellent example to help you learn the art of fruit and vegetable gardening.

Parcevall Hall Gardens, Skyreholme, North Yorkshire, BD23 6DE (www.parcevallhallgardens.co.uk) – a wonderful garden in the heart of Wharfedale with both formal and informal gardens, rockeries, woodland plantings etc. Visit RHS Harlow Carr whilst you are in the area.

RHS Garden Harlow Carr, Harrogate, HG3 1QB (www.rhs.org.uk/harlowcarr) – established in 1950 by the Northern Horticultural Society (now no longer in existence), this garden, now owned and managed by the RHS, has evolved over recent years and is now one of the best gardens in North Yorkshire, with a full events programme and many new garden features to enjoy and learn from.

Ripon Walled Garden, Palace Road, Ripon, HG4 3HN (www.riponwalledgarden.org.uk) – a garden, nursery and café in the walled garden of the old Bishop's Palace estate. Its work includes supporting and training adults with learning difficulties. A collection of old apple varieties is one of its features.

Scampston Walled Garden, Malton, North Yorkshire, YO17 8NG (www.scampston.co.uk) – an excellent example of a Piet Oudolf designed garden, with a perennial meadow as one of the main attractions.

Sheffield Botanic Gardens, Clarkehouse Road, Sheffield, S10 2LN (www.sbg.org.uk) - a horticultural oasis in a busy city. With a new visitor's centre and a restored glass pavilions, the gardens are worthy of a visit in any season.

Stillingfleet Lodge Garden, Stewart Lane, Stillingfleet, York, YO19 6HP (www.stillingfleetlodgenurseries.co.uk) – an award-winning garden with an extensive nursery selling many of the plants found in the garden. A must do garden to put on your 'bucket' list.

Thorp Perrow Arboretum and Woodland Garden, Bedale, North Yorkshire, DL8 2PR (www.thorpperrow.com) – one of the largest private collections of trees and shrubs in the north. Spectacular all year round but spring and autumn provide some brilliant highlights.

Wallington, Morpeth, Northumberland, NE61 4AR (www.nationaltrust.org.uk) – a tranquil garden that will encourage you to garden with nature rather than against it.

York Gate, Back Church Lane, Leeds, LS16 8DW (www.perennial.org.uk) – a delightful 0.4 hectare (1 acre) garden divided into 'garden rooms' that has wonderful design ideas for us all to take into our own gardens. Managed by the Perennial charity.

Yorkshire Arboretum, Castle Howard, York, YO60 7BY (www.yorkshirearboretum.org) - 48.5 hectares with more than 6000 trees from around the world to see and enjoy along with wild flower meadows to be amazed by in summer. The Castle Howard estate, house and gardens are close by (www.castlehoward.co.uk)

Yorkshire Lavender, Terrington, York, YO60 6PB (www.yorkshirelavender.com) – a 24.2 hectare garden, nursery, sculpture park and restaurant specialising in Lavenders.

Bibliography

NOTE: NOT ALL of the following books are mentioned in the book but many have been read by me in the lead-up to and writing of the book, adding to my knowledge and understanding of the complexities of trying to garden with Mother Nature rather than fighting against her.

Adams, C.R., Bamford K.M., Early M. P. 1999. *Principles of Horticulture (Third Edition)*. Butterworth-Heinemann.

Allaby, Michael. 2006. *Oxford Dictionary of Plant Sciences*. Oxford University Press.

Ayres, Alistair. 1990. *The Gardening from Which? Gardening Without Chemicals*. Consumer Association and Hodder and Stoughton.

Baines, Chris Dr. 1988. *How to make a Wildlife Garden*. Elm Tree Books.

Baines, Chris Dr. 2016. *RHS Companion to Wildlife Gardening*. Francis Lincoln Limited Publishers.

Baumgardt, John Philip. 1999. *How to Identify Flowering Plant Families – A Practical Guide for Horticulturists and Plant Lovers*. Timber Press.

Beeton, Mrs. 1985. *The Beeton Book of Garden Management*. Omega Books Ltd.

Boland, Maureen and Bridget. 1977. *Old Wive's Lore for Gardeners*. The Bodley Head Ltd.

Books TAJ. 1989. Green and Pleasant Land – *Poetry of the English Countryside*. Selectabook.

Bricknell, Christopher and Joyce David. 2011. *RHS Pruning and Training*. Dorling Kindersley.

Brown, Deni. 2008. *The Royal Horticultural Society Encyclopedia of Herbs*. Dorling Kindersley.

Bruges, James. 2000. *The Little Earth Book*. Alastair Sawday Publishing.

Buczacki, Stefan and Harris, Keith. 2005. *Pests, Diseases & Disorders of Garden Plants*. Harper Collins.

Campbell-Culver, Maggie. 2004. *The Origin of Plants*. Transworld Publishers – Eden Project Books.

Carson, Rachel. 2000. *Silent Spring*. Penguin Classics.

Carter, D.J. and Hargreaves B. 1986. *A Field Guide to Caterpillars of Butterflies and Moths in Britain and Europe*. London (Collins).

Chevallier MNIMH, Andrew. 1996. *The Encyclopedia of Medicinal Plants*. Dorling Kindersley.

Chinery, Michael. 1986. *Garden Creepy Crawlies*. Whittet Books.

Chinery, Michael. 1977. *The Natural History of the Garden*. William Collins Sons and Co Ltd.

Colborn, Theo, Dumanoski, Dianne & Myers, John Peterson. 1997. *Our Stolen Future*. Abacus.

Cubey, Janet (Editor-in-Chief). 2010-2011. *RHS Plant Finder 2010–2011* (updated every two years). Dorling Kindersley.

Darwin, Charles. 2011. *The Origin of Species*. Harper Collins Publishers.

Dawkins, Richard.2009. *The Greatest Show on Earth – The Evidence for Evolution.* Black Swan.

DEFRA 2014. National Pollinator Strategy. www.gov.uk/publications .

Elliott, Charles. 2000. *The Quotable Gardener.* London (Metro Books).

Elliott, Charles. 2006. *More Papers from the Potting Shed.* Frances Lincoln Ltd.

Elliott, Charles. 2011. *This is the Garden, An Anthology.* Frances Lincoln Ltd.

Elphick, Jonathan and Woodward, John. 2009. *RSPB Pocket Birds of Britain and Europe.* Dorling Kindersley.

Enson, Paul. 2009. *Yorkshire Geology.* The Dovecote Press.

Fitter, Alistair. 1987. *Collins New Generation Guide Wild Flowers of Britain and Northern Europe.* Collins.

Flowerdew, Bob. 2004. *Complete Book of Companion Planting.* Kyle Books.

Foggitt, William. 1978. *Weather Book.* Chorley (Countryside Publications Ltd.)

Foggitt, Bill and Markham Len. 1993. *The Yorkshire Weather Book.* (Countryside Books.)

Grigson, Geoffrey. 1974. *A Dictionary of English Plant Names.* Allan Lane, (a division of Penguin Books Ltd)

Hart, Robert A.de J. 1994. *Forest Gardening.* Green Books.

Heaney, Seamus. 1998. *Opened Ground Poems 1966–1996. Faber* and Faber.

Hills, Lawrence D. 1989. *Fighting Like the Flowers.* Green Books.

Holmgren, David. 2002. *Permaculture: Principles and Pathways Beyond Sustainability.* Holmgren Design Services.

Huxley, Anthony. 1999. *The New Royal Horticultural Society Dictionary of Gardening.* London (Macmillan Reference Limited).

Ingram, David S., Vince-Prue Daphne, Gregory Peter J. 2002. *Science and the Garden.* Blackwell Publishing.

Jordan, Michael. 1995. *The Encylopedia of Fungi of Britain and Europe.* David and Charles.

Maiden Joe. 2010. *Grow with Joe.* Great Northern Books.

Marinelli, Janet (Editor-in-Chief). 2004. *Plant.* Dorling Kindersley.

Mitchell, Michael. 2011. *Alpines, An Essential Guide.* The Crowood Press.

Moore, Helen. 2015. *Ecozoa.* Permanent Publications.

Moore, Thomas. 1997. *The Re-Enchantment of Everyday Life.* Hodder and Stoughton.

Osler, Mirabel. 1989. *A Gentle Plea for Chaos – reflections from an English Garden.* Bloomsbury.

Page, Robin. 1977. *Weather Forecasting the Country Way.* Penguin Books Ltd.

Pears, Pauline (Editor-in-Chief). 2001. *Encyclopaedia of Organic Gardening.* Dorling Kindersley.

Pilcher, Michael, Davis Lisa, Hurrion David. 1995. *Garden Terms.* Hamlyn.

Pollock, Michael. 2002. *RHS Fruit and Vegetable Gardening.* Dorling Kindersley.

Preben, Bang and Preben, Dahlstrom. 1980. *Collins Guide to Animal tracks and signs.* Glasgow (Collins).

Quest-Ritson, Charles and Brigid. 2011. *The Royal Horticultural Society Encyclopedia of Roses.* Dorling Kindersley.

Robinson, Peter. 1998. *The Royal Horticultural Society Water Gardening.* Dorling Kindersley.

Robinson, William. 1900. *English Flower Garden and Home Grounds.* John Murray.

Shepherd, Allen. 2007. *The Little Book of Compost.* Collins.

Shepherd, Allen and Galant, Suzanne. 2002. *The Little Book of Slugs.* CAT Publications.

Spencer-Jones, Rae (Editor-in-Chief). 2007. *1001 GARDENS YOU MUST SEE BEFORE YOU DIE.* Cassell Illustrated.

Stearn, William T. 1998. *Botanical Latin (Fourth Edition).* David and Charles.

Thomas, Graham Stuart. 1982. *Perennial Garden Plants. (or The Modern Florilegium)* J.M. Dent and Sons Ltd.

Thomas, Graham Stuart. 1989. *The Rock Garden and its Plants – from Grotto to Alpine House.* J. M. Dent & Sons Ltd.

Tompkins, Peter and Bird, Christopher. 1974. *The Secret Life of Plants.* Penguin Books Ltd.

Van, Zyl Miezan. 2009. *Wildlife of Britain.* Dorling Kindersley.

White, Reverend Gilbert. 1789 and 1984. *The Illustrated Natural History of Selbourne.* Macmillan.

Wilson-Rich, Noah. 2014. *The Bee. A Natural History.* Ivy Press.

Wong, James. 2010. *Grow your own Drugs.* Collins.

Woodward, Anthony and Penn, Robert. 2007 *The Wrong Kind of Snow.* Hodder & Stoughton.

Dedication

THIS BOOK IS firstly, and most importantly, dedicated to my dear wife Judy, who has had to suffer my ramblings, grumblings and chunterings over recent years as this book has unfolded from a tiny seed of an idea, formed when I was but a mere slip of a lad in my fifties, to its present state. Without her love and support, my professional career would not have followed the path that it has and I might never have taken on the writing of a weekly gardening article in our local newspaper, the Huddersfield Daily Examiner, in 1999, let alone taking on the role of Gardening Expert on BBC Radio Leeds in 2015 after the sad demise of Joe Maiden. It is through these processes that my ideas on where gardening has gone and might be going have been more finely tuned to the point where I feel confident enough to share my thoughts and ideas with a wider audience.

Secondly, I would also like to dedicate this book to my two daughters, Gillian and Nicola and my four beautiful grandchildren, Adam, Libby, Thomas and Jacob in the hope that the world that we gift to them is a little more peaceful, safe, stable and sustainable than when it was given to us and that they can help to ensure a healthier future for the planet and future generations as yet unseen and unknown.

I would also like to mention Dr. Chris Baines, whose inspirational wildlife gardening series, 'Blue Tits and Bumblebees,' on BBC television in the early 1980s made me think more deeply about the path that I and many other professional horticulturists and agriculturists had been treading since the Second World War, when the enthusiasm for ripping hedgerows out, filling in farm ponds and spraying anything that moved got under way – this attitude was handed on to amateur gardeners by default, as the modern range of inorganic chemicals began to appear in garden centres from the 1950s onwards. In addition, Rachel Carson's book Silent Spring, written some years after this post-war madness got underway, made me realise the damage that we have caused to our world, albeit sometimes without realising it until it is too late.

As a supporter of the two hospices (Kirkwood Hospice and West Yorkshire Forget-Me-Not Trust) in the Huddersfield area, I will be gifting 5% of all profits made from the sale of this book to them to assist them in their wonderful work with sick adults and children and their families.

Many thanks to Jeremy Mills and his staff for having enough faith in me to finally complete this book.